THE BARTER BOOK

THE
BARTER
·BOOK

Dyanne Asimow Simon

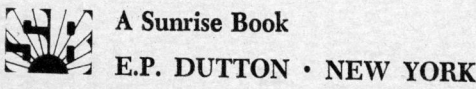

A Sunrise Book

E.P. DUTTON · NEW YORK

To my mother and father, who always paid cash

A Rose & Asseyev Project

For information contact:
E.P. Dutton, 2 Park Avenue, New York, NY 10016

Library of Congress Cataloging in Publication Data

Simon, Dyanne Asimow.
    The barter book.

    Bibliography: p.
    1. Barter. 2. Commerce. I. Title.
HF1007.S494 1979 381 78-16928

ISBN: 0-87690-290-5-pbk.
ISBN: 0-87690-352-9

Published simultaneously in Canada by
Clarke, Irwin & Company Limited, Toronto and Vancouver

10 9 8 7 6 5 4 3 2 1

First Edition

Contents

THE BARTER BOOK

1

An Introduction to Barter

"I have a proposition! You take my Windjammer Cruises and I'll take those Vegas hotel rooms off your hands!"

The speaker, a middle-aged executive in Los Angeles, was negotiating long distance with a Florida franchise. His bulbous nose, stuck onto his face like an afterthought, glowed red with energy. He strutted. He cajoled. He performed for the phone.

"I've got folks crying for a vacation at the Dunes."

Computer read-outs were stacked on his desk. Electronic equipment lined the walls.

"I'm doing you a favor. Windjammer Cruises are A—Number One items!"

His office had a view. Ensconced in a crescent column of tinted glass, it shot high over the La Brea tar pits for a panorama of Southern California sprawl. But he never looked.

"What do I want?" His face contorted, as though in pain. "I want the rooms at the Dunes! Singles, doubles, I don't care. Throw in the Cary Grant Suite—I'll love you forever!"

He could have been in a crowded stall in an ancient marketplace. Unravel his doubleknit, put him in a caftan— Los Angeles businessman transformed to Moroccan haggler

—trading Windjammer Cruises for last year's camel saddles and winding up with fifty pounds of pure Spanish saffron to boot. The man was a barterer. His love of the game transcended time and space.

"I'm telling you, I can't move those cruises. Folks out here don't want to fly to Florida to get on a boat. But Vegas is close. Give me the rooms and they'll go like hotcakes!"

The deal was completed. He was pleased. He could parlay those rooms into advertising space and a manufacturer's close-out on restaurant hardware. His fingers were already dialing. A triple play was on the way.

Before the end of the year, this man and his colleagues will have negotiated $12 million worth of business, all through barter.

Barter is fast taking over the imagination of the practical American people. Reports from newspapers and magazines across the country indicate that barter is a mushrooming phenomenon. The *Chicago Tribune,* the *Albuquerque Journal, The New York Times,* the *Mobile Press Register,* the *Los Angeles Times, The Capitalist Reporter, The Wall Street Journal, New York* magazine, *Time, Business Week, Mother Earth News,* NBC, and CBS all have noted the proliferation of barter organizations within the past year. It is estimated that at least eight million Americans practice some form of barter in their everyday lives.

Senior citizens and car dealers are joining trade exchanges. So are typists and parachutists. Just as Lillian Hellman and Diana Ross are reported to have bartered their appearance in a Blackgama ad for a Blackgama coat, and Francis Ford Coppola bartered a copy of the film *Godfather 2* for the chance to meet Fidel Castro, so Joann McCrakin of Useful Services Exchange in Reston, Virginia, polishes silver in exchange for fresh vegetables and repairs on her antique clock. Top restaurants, such as The Four Seasons and The Grand Central Oyster Bar in New York and Lawry's in Los Angeles, routinely have traded meal credit for publicity. Now, through barter clubs, veterinarians and optometrists can trade their services for meals at restaurants as well.

People from all walks of life are bartering. And for good reasons! Barter is a way to:

1. Beat inflation
2. Avoid taxes
3. Save money
4. Get bargains
5. Increase business
6. Make acquaintances
7. Have fun
8. Personalize commercial transactions
9. Assert more control over economic life
10. Integrate economics with social and ecological values

Though bartering is nothing new, its resurgence in popularity is. The IRS has no way to estimate the amount of bartering taking place; neither do business groups, chambers of commerce, or trade-regulation agencies. All they know is that "it's happening," and that it is happening with greater frequency this year than it was last year or the year before.

Although no statistics reveal how many people exchange roses for widgets, the Stanford Research Institute (SRI) recently published a report for the business community about a trend it calls "voluntary simplicity." This refers to people who are "living a life that is outwardly simple but inwardly rich"; a life that embraces material simplicity, human scale, self-determination, ecological awareness, and personal growth. Bartering is harmonious with all five categories. It is a means of exchange often employed by these people.

Using SRI statistics, we can add "barter" to "voluntary simplicity" (VS) and approximate the number of VS barterers and barter sympathizers.

| | Maximum Growth of VS (millions of adults) | | |
	1977	1987	2000
Full VS	5	25	60
Partial VS	10	35	60
Sympathizers	60	50	25
Indifferent	75	60	55

We can add to those statistics those hundreds of thousands of barter-club members who are attracted not by the social or philosophical aspects of barter, but by the additional leeway barter gives to the concept of income and its subsequent tax advantages. (Note to the reader: the information in this book relating to income tax and barter transactions is necessarily general. The reader is urged to call his or her tax adviser with specific questions about barter clubs or income tax statements—especially insofar as local taxes are concerned.)

Barter clubs are organizations which capitalize on this fact by creating a method of indirect trade. A can trade with B without B's having to trade with A. Using computers, the clubs record all trades and keep track of all credit and debit. They cater to professionals, businesses, and services. The idea was born in California twenty years ago, but the 1970s have seen it spread to almost every state in the union, particularly Utah, Florida, Nevada, Washington, Minnesota, and Illinois. The major clubs, such as Business Exchange and Mutual Credit Buying Systems (both of California) and Unlimited Business Exchange and Exchange Enterprises (both of Utah) have franchise operations not only in this country, but also in England, New Zealand, Australia, Canada, Japan, and Germany.

There remains a wide range of people falling between the philosophic barterers of voluntary simplicity and the economic barterers of maximum profit. They live everywhere. They do everything. They cannot be classified by any one trait, except that many of them belong to the middle class.

Back in the good old days, the middle class believed in hard cash. Barter was for the poor, who could not afford to buy. Barter was for the superrich, who owned everything and traded it among themselves. Barter was for country doctors getting paid with chickens, for kids with trading cards and bottle caps, something natives did in jungles.

Barter, "the trade or exchange of goods or services without the use of money," was unsettling to the middle class. Earlier linguistic connotations lingered on. The old French *barater:* to barter, to cheat. The Vulgar Latin, *prattare:* to cheat. Cash was less messy. The middle class could afford to buy what it wanted, and that was what earning a living was all about.

Times have changed. Suddenly, the cost-of-living index is going wild. Prices have gone up. Taxes have gone up. Employment has gone down. Affluence has acquired a peaked appearance. Alarm spreads from laid-off aerospace engineers to Giorgio's of Beverly Hills. How are people to pay their debts? They have no cash. In California, millions respond to Governor Jerry Brown's dictum "less is more," not because that is what they want, but because that is what they are getting. The dollar buys very little.

The middle class is realizing that it must throw off centuries of bourgeois conditioning and reevaluate its commercial habits. People are beginning to do just that. They are coming up with a more economic, more pleasurable, more meaningful alternative—barter.

Mary Addison is one of them. Somewhere in the tangle of freeways which knit Orange County together, Mary's safety-yellow Austin Mini died. That was it! She could not afford any more repairs on her beloved but unpredictable car. It had to be towed to Maurice the mechanic.

"What can I do?" wailed Mary, a designer, who understood the intricacies of laying out ads and printing magazines far better than the intricacies of her Mini's motor. "We have no money! We owe our dentist for the last visits, our plumber for the leaky faucets. . . ."

"And me," interrupted Maurice, "for the last repair job."

Mary slumped onto the nearest transmission. The manila folder in her hands dropped to the ground. Sketches for Los Angeles Philharmonic stationery she was designing flew in every direction. She was at her lowest ebb.

Maurice sympathetically retrieved the sketches. As he wiped grease spots off them, it occurred to him that the one thing he had always wanted was classy stationery that would increase his status in the small but competitive world of foreign-auto mechanics.

Mary Addison rejoiced. Her Mini was saved. Barter was the answer!

That night, Mary told her husband, Larry, what had happened. She was designing Maurice's stationery in exchange for repairs on their car. They wouldn't have to pay a cent.

Larry Addison, a terrific tennis player and no fool, immediately called Dr. Jones, their pudgy dentist. Larry exchanged ten tennis lessons for two past-due prophylaxis bills. Mary, inspired by her success with Maurice, convinced their plumber that his ads in the local paper needed revamping.

The Addisons had discovered barter as a way out of their financial crunch. And not only did it ease their finances, it provided unexpected benefits as well. Larry's accounting practice increased. Mary found more free-lance clients. Seeking opportunities for barter challenged their imagination and made them feel self-sufficient. Most of all, bartering was fun! Business transactions ceased to be cut and dried. Personal relationships developed, making the transactions more meaningful. They told their friends. The circle of enthusiasts grew. They had created a bartering community.

How did they do it?

People know that Queen Isabella gave Columbus three ships and he gave her America. They know that Peter Minuit gave Indians blankets and beads and they gave him Manhattan. They might even know that Cézanne, Van Gogh, and Picasso traded their work for art supplies, eventually making their "benefactors" very rich.

But bartering today, for those who do not do it, is a somewhat mysterious process. People have a lot of questions about it.

How does it *really* work? Do you need special skills? Don't you get gypped? How do you know what to barter, or what it's worth? Where do you meet other barterers? What are the barter clubs? How are they organized? Does barter make a difference in anyone's life?

These are the kind of questions this book will answer. It is not an encyclopedia of barter, nor is it an academic study of the sociology of barter. Rather, it is an introduction to this fascinating subject, an overview of the people who do it, the structures they use, the philosophies they espouse, and how we can apply this information to our own lives.

Because barter can make a difference.

The people who barter know. They live in communities with support networks. They fight an overgrown, competitive, wasteful dollar economy with small but effective trades. They recycle. They do not hoard. They share. Instead of being the victims of price fixing, they control the value of their own goods and services. To these people, economics is a game. They have fun with barter. They are willing to seize the moment and go with it. They trust their intuitions. Flexibility and imagination are more important than dollar signs. Their sense of adventure leads them to new people, new possibilities.

We, too, can be barter people. After all, not so many years have passed since we identified with Jack as he met an old man with a handful of beans, traded his cow, and began one of the great adventures of all time.

2.

A Brief Look
at Barter
in the Past

In the fourteenth century, Ibn Batuta, an Arab traveler, described a form of trade which he said occurred in the far northern "Land of Darkness." Merchants deposited goods as evening fell in a certain location in the wild. During the night, natives came, took what they found and left "skins of sable, miniver and ermine." In the morning, the merchants would check the furs. If they were satisfied, they would take them; if not, they would leave them. The next day they would find that more skins had been added, or that their original pile of goods had been returned.

This is known as "silent trade," and examples exist the world over.

The act holds mystery for us. How do people know what to leave? Why are they silent? Was there some historical hostility between them? Some great cultural and linguistic barrier?

When we think of trade, we think of social interaction; we don't think of silent peoples leaving piles of goods unattended in the wilderness.

This is interesting; the thrust of nineteenth- and early twentieth-century economics was to isolate economics and study it as a science unto itself. With its mathematical equations, market-system analysis, and projective charts, it became as silent and unresponsive as the pile of skins in the land of darkness, waiting to be accepted or rejected by native merchants.

Along with this scientific and rational approach to economics came a new set of assumptions—namely, that gift exchange, barter, and money were three phases in the evolution of economics, with money representing the last and most sophisticated phase.

However, anthropological and historical evidence has recently demonstrated that this is not so. Money, rather than developing as a latter-day method to facilitate trade, probably evolved much earlier, serving noncommercial and ceremonial purposes. Cattle, pigs, and shells (all "money") were used to purchase brides; shells, pigs, and cloth to pay initiation fees. The Phoenicians, the leading traders of their period, did not use money, even though other peoples of the time did.

A look at many societies reveals a multiplicity of economic methods. Gift exchange, barter, and money often exist side by side, operating simultaneously, playing different, though interdependent, roles.

In ancient Mesopotamia, the accounts of city temples were kept by means of silver coins, yet the payment was made in oil and barley. For the Tiv, a people living in central Nigeria, money (in the form of brass rods) and barter played complementary roles through the 1950s. Brass rods were used to purchase prestige items such as cattle and ritual offices. But to use them for food, something grown by each family for its own consumption and/or traded at the market, was a sign of failure. And although brass rods were used in establishing goodwill, and it was considered a sign of success if a man could convert brass-rod wealth into wives and daughters, properly speaking, to the Tiv, the only true payment for a woman was a woman.

And, in Malinowski's famous study of the Trobriand Islanders, a Melanasian tribe, a variety of overlapping systems of exchange are observed:

1. Pure gifts
2. Customary payments, repaid irregularly and without strict equivalence

3. Payment for services rendered
4. Gifts returned in economically equivalent form
5. Exchange of material goods against privileges, titles, and nonmaterial possessions
6. Ceremonial barter, with deferred payment
7. Trade pure and simple

The Trobriand Islanders use the word *kula* to indicate reciprocal gift exchange of prestige items such as necklaces and bracelets made of shells. *Kula* is accompanied by elaborate social ritual and assumes enormous status implications. The word *gimwali* signifies the barter of subsistence goods between random buyers and sellers who have no social relationship with each other. There is much haggling over value; both parties try to get a bargain. It is improper to conduct *kula* as though it were *gimwali*.

Although *gimwali* exists, most subsistence items, such as yams and fish, are exchanged through gift-giving reciprocity based on kinship obligations. Malinowski says that "the whole tribal life is permeated by a constant give and take; that every ceremony, every legal and customary act is done to the accompaniment of material gifts and counter gifts."

Malinowski's description of the Trobriand Islanders was seminal in the development of economic anthropology. It illuminated the principle that economic relationships are embedded in social ones.

"The views that the native can live in a state of individual search for food, or catering for his own household only, in isolation from any interchange of goods implies a calculating, cold egotism. . . . These views ignore the fundamental human impulse to display, to share, to bestow. They ignore the deep tendency to create social ties through exchange of gifts" (Malinowski, *Argonauts of the Western Pacific*).

The gifts are not free of expectation and obligation. On the contrary, embodied within the gift itself, particularly *kula* items, is a spiritual essence dictating that the item not be hoarded, that it be passed on. Once they get them, the Trobrianders do not keep their highly valued, precious *kula* necklaces or bracelets. They go on long and sometimes dangerous journeys to make sure that these items are passed on. If they were to keep them, the Trobrianders would lose all social respect and be demeaned. By going to such lengths to keep *kula* a living part of their social structure, they are able to ensure continuity, stability, and a transmission of values—all necessary for the health of a viable society.

The economics of the Trobriand Islands is multicentric; that is, there are different but overlapping circles of exchange. This is assumed to be an aspect of primitive societies, but not of our own. We, presumably, have a distinct market system which can be separated from our society as a whole and studied independently.

The truth of this remains debatable. It is certainly difficult to look at our economic behavior with the eye of a Malinowski; but if we move back, even a step, from our involvement with the stock market, bank accounts, and cost-of-living indexes, we can see evidence that all is not as isolated as it seems. We, too, have overlapping circles of exchange. Though the dollar dominates our economic landscape, we employ both barter and gift exchange in our everyday transactions.

Why do we feel put upon if someone fails to return our hospitality? How do we determine how much to spend on wedding presents? To whom do we give liquor at Christmas time?

A gift is not something freely given. It carries with it expectation and obligation. Another anthropologist points out that a gift "at most is a venture, a hopeful speculation." We use it to lubricate social situations. Generosity is as much a sign of wealth and status in our society as it is for the Trobrianders. Exchange insures social continuity. When you move into a new neighborhood and borrow a cup of sugar, you are doing more than getting sugar. You are beginning a relationship. Our grandparents knew this. Newcomers were greeted with baked goods or a bottle of wine. These gifts were returned in kind. A continuity of relationship was insured.

We must distinguish between gift exchange and barter. Like *kula,* gift exchange in our society occurs among people who already know each other and know their respective status delineations. Gifts have a vocabulary of their own, much of it not rational, but understood nonetheless. We do not give the boss's wife a negligee, nor a Mercedes to our local representative. We respect the boundaries within gift exchange; it becomes a way of keeping goods within a certain social segment.

Barter, like *gimwali*, often occurs between strangers. Goods are traded between social sectors which otherwise would have no particular personal contact. In fact, as is evident at flea markets, swap meets, and trade shows, barter is a way for diverse groups to intermingle much the way they used to at the medieval markets in Europe, or today in the casbahs of North Africa or the *mercados* of Latin America. Social status is not an issue. Everyone is after a bargain.

To get their bargains, people interact. They cajole, they threaten, they shout, they plead, they charm. Casbahs and *mercados* are not silent, lonely places. Nor are trade shows or flea markets. The air is filled with sounds of people, a spectacle of human acitivy. There is an aura of excitement that you do not find as you wait in line at the bank with your withdrawal or deposit slips.

Barter occurs between friends and neighbors as well. When you trade off baby-sitting and rides to the office or when you exchange your never-used yogurt maker for a friend's toaster, you are bartering.

With gift exchange, value equivalence is implicit and timing is a matter of sensitivity. There is an etiquette which proscribes that gift giving should not look like a direct exchange. The lapse of time between gifts keeps the balance uneven and keeps the give and take of the relationship going.

Barter is not as subtle. I do for you. You do for me. I like that. You like this. Let's exchange. It falls between the intimacy and sensitivity of gift exchange, with its somewhat formal status-conscious boundaries, and the abstract impersonality of dollars. It can play an intermediary role in a society like ours, which no longer is satisfied with its Victorian version of silent trade, that scientific model of exchange which excludes social relationships from its construct.

There are times when barter suggests gift giving. It is personal, responsive, and yet unburdened by some of the protocal which makes gift giving lose meaning in large, complex, and mobile social units. At other times, barter resembles money. It is a way of doing business. A way of getting value. The history of barter often demonstrates that certain barter items are traded with such regularity that they become accepted as a standard means of payment.

This happened in colonial America when England prevented her colonies from minting their own currency. Tobacco and beaver skins became widely accepted as units of payment. Beaver skins were such a universal form of money that the Hudson Bay Company issued copper beaver-shaped tokens which were circulated at the value of one skin each.

Today, in certain circles, drugs and guns, though not officially sanctioned as legal tender, have become acceptable payment for services rendered.

One record producer who prefers to remain anonymous says that cocaine is "the most common barter in the industry." Cocaine is often broken down into one gram for three hours of studio kickback time—a complex bookkeeping method that gives the producer off-the-books money spent by the studio for recording time in the form of cocaine.

According to *The Wall Street Journal,* hand guns are a more secure investment than anything but gold and silver. Because the demand is greater than the supply, they never go down in value. They can and are traded to get anything—from property to dental care.

At gun shows, such as those held in the Great Western Exhibition Hall of Los Angeles, there exists a trading fervor equal only to that of market day in Toluca, Mexico. Hundreds of people mill about, mostly men. Adorned with tatoos, jewelry, ornate belt buckles, they represent every walk of life. At one table sits a man who traded $250,000 worth of property in Newport Beach for a pile of antique guns and came out ahead. At another table is an old European immigrant, displaying pocket watches and rare Quackenbush Herkimer bicycle pistols. There are off-duty policemen, beer-bellied hunters, long-haired hippies, Chicago businessmen, auto mechanics, and advertising executives. They all know gun values. They all like to trade.

.And so they walk around, examining guns. Though there are arrowheads, squash-blossom necklaces, and South American hatchets, guns are the favored barter item. Laden with cultural content, embued with macho symbolism, guns are polished, caressed, and admired.

The equation gun = good investment = acceptable means of payment in lieu of money =favored barter item = symbolic cultural object traded from one person to the next, illustrates the workings of nonrational behavior in our own economic lives.

It is a fiction that we can perform economic transactions as though we were engaged in silent trade. Though our banks are impersonal, anonymous institutions and our credit cards, checks, and money transfers do not require much in the way of human contact, we trespass the limits of this particular exchange system every day. The give and take which permeates primitive society can and does permeate our own.

For a long time economists ignored this fact, embarrassed by their inability to make economics a pure science. But not any more. With all the "loosening" of society and its structures that has emerged in the last decade, we no longer seek a form of pure economics divested of human connection. Rather, we acknowledge the connection and seek ways to affirm it. Barter is one way. It is a means of exchange that creates social ties, insures continuity of relationships, and provides a peaceful and more generous method of dealing with status and power.

METHODS OF BARTER

How do people barter in our society? How do they make a profit? How do they achieve equal value? How do they create support networks or use barter to achieve social change? In what ways do people barter individually? Collectively?

There are probably as many ways to barter as there are to love. Major bartering patterns fall into the following classifications:

1. *Individual swap* or *equal-value trade*—the most prevalent form of barter, the kind most of us have done at least once in our lives
2. *Community barter*—a nonstructured support system based on a lot of sharing and giving and taking between members of the same community
3. *Networks and exchanges*—organized forms of information distribution enabling strangers to trade on a non-profit basis
4. *Horsetrading* or *trading up*—an individual form of barter, with intention to make profit
5. *Barter clubs*—a relatively new form of organized trading, primarily for businesses and professionals, with a profit orientation

These categories are by no means pure. Characteristics from one frequently cross over to another. For example, individuals who engage in horsetrading share many characteristics with individuals who trade for equal value. Though one might be after a profit and the other after an even exchange, they both relish the moves of the game. Equal-value swappers as well as horsetraders compare barter to chess and Monopoly; they like the mental stimulation of matching wits and they appreciate a good opponent.

A well-known pop sculptor and artist, J. finds himself turning from horsetrader to equal-value trader if he is particularly satisfied with a deal he's just made. "Barter's a game," he says, "a contest. An emotional exchange. Many times after I've made an exceptional trade, at the end I'll give the other guy something worth twice as much, just because I've enjoyed the experience."

On the other hand, the various forms of group exchange offer a different crossing over of characteristics. Though quite diverse in social, political, and economic attitudes, they share an organizational approach which makes it possible for people to integrate barter into their lives in some structured, predictable fashion. Moreover, they tend to attract people who want to incorporate barter into larger schemes.

Tom Skala, president of a large Los Angeles barter club, Mutual Credit Buying Systems, is an aggressive entrepreneurial figure who envisions a cashless society webbed with interlocking computerized trade. He has nothing in common with John Vasconcellos, a humanistic assemblyman in the California state legislature, except the latter's belief that barter groups and networks present a new and exciting alternative for conventional systems of exchange—in Vasconcellos's case, the exchange being of information, services, and the sharing of political power.

The question of intent provides for further overlapping among barter categories. Horsetrading and barter clubs exist to make profit, not to transform economic values. Equal-value swapping, community reciprocity, networks and exchanges do question economic values and attempt to transform them at one level or another.

Barter clubs have the hint of the con and the glint of the game, the aura of successful traders who started with fish hooks and wound up with empires. Networks and exchanges have their roots in religious, ethical, and political tradition, and reflect the barn-raising spirit of bygone days.

Both are typically American. Our history, our mythology are full of tales of individual self-reliance and clever skullduggery on the one hand, and community cohesiveness and neighborly support on the other. The one does not preclude the other. We admire both and fluctuate between the two.

We will divide the discussion of barter methods into two sections: individual barter and collective barter.

First of all, we will take a look at the granddaddy of all profit barter, the horsetrader.

3.

Individual Barter

HORSETRADING

Horsetrader is a generic term for anyone who engages in shrewd and vigorous bargaining. Descended from gypsy thieves and Yankee peddlers, horsetraders are notorious in literature and life for their sharp deals, tricks, and conniving charm. Paying no heed to prevailing economic systems, they roamed their way through history, honing the art of barter as they provided necessary goods and desirable luxuries to the root-bound on the farms and in the villages of the world.

Scott Melville, a beefy, genial man of fifty-five who calls Tombstone, Arizona, his home, was trained in the business as a youth. He traveled the Oklahoma-Arkansas-Texas circuit with a covered wagon and a string of doctored horses. By the time he was twelve, Scott knew how to fix an old mare's teeth, stain gray hairs, treat short-windedness and plump out gaunt bellies. He could "snide" the people because he never saw them again.

To hear Scott tell it, each trade was a masterstroke. "Everybody's looking to steal something. It's like playing poker!" And he always came out with the straight flush.

Scott doesn't trade horses anymore. He trades pickup

trucks and motor homes. He claims to play fair. But, as he pats his wide girth and acknowledges how he's making a good living, the gleam in his eye gives him away.

Whether horsetraders are into horses or cars, job lots or oil paintings, they know how to seize advantage. And their trade always goes in one direction—up! *Trading up is the cardinal rule.* It is the source of the challenge, the secret of success. Two horsetraders trying to best each other are a sight to behold. Engaged in a mental duel, they thrust, parry, bow respectfully before the other's expertise, then go for the jugular. It is a matter of professional pride that they come away from a deal having traded up.

Trading up simply means that what you've gotten is worth more than what you traded. But simple is not the way horsetraders like to keep it. They don't trade up once and let it go at that. They parlay their gain into something worth even more. They pyramid, topping the last deal with the next deal. For horsetraders, it's the action of the deal that counts, and they follow it through the way crapshooters follow the run of the dice.

"It's the deal. If I don't have a deal, man, I can hardly get out of bed. But if I got a deal, I can go without eating, without sex, without movies—because I got a deal," pronounces Robbie Owens, a large blond man in his thirties, dressed in a T-shirt and patched jeans.

Robbie considers himself a horsetrader par excellence. He is married and has two children. His wife has gone back to college. They live in Van Nuys, a section of the great sunbrowned stain that is southern California's San Fernando Valley. It is the domain of wrecked car parts, decaying stucco, smog, and a wide, flat monotony broken only by motorcycles, RVs, and shopping centers.

Like many traders' homes, Robbie's is piled high with junk. The lawn is scarcely visible beneath old cars, machinery, appliances, and rusting mattress springs. A large gray-blue shell of a boat sits near the curb. In the back, a flying saucer, presumably once used by Ringo Starr, nests among ivy, generators, and old bikes. Robbie deliberately keeps his house a dumping ground. It is important for his reputation. It makes it easier for people to come by with things to trade.

Most traders like to brag about their successes, the pyramids which started from scratch and finished high in the air. Robbie is certainly no exception. He'll readily tell you about the time he traded forty-eight boxes of nails, worth $650, for a Lincoln Continental, and the Lincoln for a $1000-MGB, $200 in parts, and $70 cash to boot.

Robbie not only brags about his deals, he is willing to tell how he engineers them—the research involved, the charades he plays, the places he goes, the moves he makes.

"When you swap, you never look like you have more than the other guy. Who wants to trade with someone who has more? I try to be the opposite of who I'm trading with. My wife gets the first view and she tells me what's coming. If soneone's wearing expensive clothes, I'll look like a bum. You've got to keep them off guard in order to have the upper hand."

There are exceptions. Sometimes it pays to look richer. Even Robbie admits that. He has a friend, Mark Vanderhill, who collects Navaho rugs. Like many collectors, he is a horse-trader in disguise. A man in Chicago had a rug Mark wanted, but would not sell it or trade it for anything except one beautiful Caucasian rug owned by a man in Cincinnati who had already promised it to his cardiologist. Mark put on his most elegant, costly attire, went to Cincinnati and pretended to be the naive scion to a tremendous cookie fortune. Taking the tack that he was willing to spend any amount, he enthused, "Money? What is money for a thing of beauty! I've got to have it!" His offer was so extravagant (yet below the actual worth of the rug) that its owner could not say no. With Caucasian rug in hand, Mark then went to his man in Chicago and exchanged it for the Navaho rug he wanted.

Robbie likes to trade with new people each time, because he feels he can make better deals with less effort. In order to keep fresh faces coming, he cultivates his image as a character, an eccentric. That way, potential customers hear about him by word of mouth. He proposes ridiculous trades. "I'll make an offer for anything. Someone gets interested, I go into an act. If there is something he wants, I say that he has what I want, even if he doesn't. I tell stories. I get him worked up. I win him over."

"You have to know when a person is bored with you," says pop artist J., who has bartered not only his artwork, but cars, horses, guns, and scrap metal. He feels that traders are always seducing. With their gift of empathy, they tune into others' needs and then sway them, manipulate them. Traders want immediate rewards, "the stroking they got from protective mamas when they couldn't get anywhere with their daddies."

Tricky as they seem, however, traders don't lie. They pride themselves on not needing to. Even on the trail, Scott Melville never lied. "I'd just tell the folks to use their eyes. I'd say, 'The horse looks good to me. How's it look to you?' "

Robbie sometimes stretches the truth, but mostly he relies on people's ignorance and slow wits. When he makes deals, he discusses things in terms of pairs—"I'll give you two of these, and throw in a pair of those"—proceeding to make the intricacies of the exchange so convoluted that the other person always has a hard time following.

He never barters for something without knowing its value. The most essential book for a trader, says Robbie, is the Sears Roebuck catalogue. You can price just about anything in it.

There are other books he finds helpful. They comprise an eclectic assortment, from getting rich quick to living off the land. He recommends the following:

ROBBIE'S BEST BOOKS

1. *How to Make It on the Land,* R. Cohan
2. *The Screwing of the Average Man,* David Hapgood
3. *You Can Find a Fortune,* Jeanne Horn
4. *How to Live on Nothing,* Joan R. Shortney
5. *Your Check Is in the Mail,* Bruce Goldman
6. *The Robber Barons,* Matthew Josephson
7. *Succeed and Grow Rich Through Persuasion,* Nap Hill
8. *Going Crazy,* R. D. Laing
9. *The Rich and the Super-Rich,* Ferdinand Lundberg
10. *How to Sell Your Way to Financial Freedom,* John Newbein
11. *The Organizers' Manual,* O. M. Collective
12. *The Art of Negotiating,* Gerard L. Nierenberg
13. *The Very Very Rich and How They Got That Way,* Max Gunter

14. *How Millionaires Made Their Fortunes and How You Can Make Yours*, Dr. R. C. Schaffer
15. *Steal This Book*, Abbie Hoffman
16. *Man, the Manipulator*, Everett L. Shostrom
17. *Great Sales by Today's Great Salesmen*, Lassor Blumenthal
18. *How to Think Like a Millionaire and Get Rich*, Howard Hill
19. *Coin Collecting as a Hobby*, Burton Hobson

Robbie never makes a deal if he doesn't get at least 100 percent profit, and he always asks for a little extra in cash. That's called *booting*. "I always ask what they'll give me to boot. That's your action, your food money."

He keeps an old, nonfunctioning Simca Huit Coupe and a Lancia Arelia parked in his yard. He would never park a new Cadillac, as that would turn people off. But the people are impressed that he can restore old cars.

"The more impressed they are by me, the better deals I can make. A lot of my stuff revolves around cars because I know about them, everybody has or wants them, and most people know nothing about them."

His garage also functions as a body shop. It is bad for a trader's reputation if he or she has no legitimate work. But Robbie spends little time in the garage. He is usually "out in the field," tracking down potential trades.

He goes to county hospital auctions, pawn shops, swap meets, flea markets, fairs, trade shows; he reads the swap columns and pays strict attention to government-surplus sales.

These sales are a surprisingly fecund source. One time, for instance, Robbie bought twenty tons of soap from the government for $240. The next week he sold half of it to a major chain, Standard Brand Paint Stores, for $6,000, and asked a friend to be his partner in distributing the other half, thereby canceling out old debts he had incurred with his friend. Then he "sold out" his partner position for 200 pounds of graphite, 38 Azimuth Information Centers, and a generator, all of which he was able to parlay into considerable profit.

Robbie is a small-time operator compared to the barter barons, those international horsetraders such as Moretin Binn of Atwood Richards and Simon Moskovics, the European "King of the Switchers," who operate on multimillion-dollar levels (see page 63). But in essence, the rules Robbie puts down for the trade remain the same for everyone:

1. Take what comes your way. You never can tell when it will come in handy.
2. Remember who has what and who needs what.
3. Keep on top of your audience. Don't let it get bored.
4. Be an expert in your field. Know prices.
5. Always get the other person to name a price first.
6. Present your trade so it appears to be to the other's advantage.
7. Make the deal complex, so only you can follow it.
8. Stay tuned in to the other person. Be what he or she is not. Size up his or her weakness and greed.
9. Make certain your profit will be sizable, or don't bother.
10. Be patient. Pyramids aren't built in a day.

THE SWAP

Not everyone has a horsetrader's instinct, nor is everyone concerned about making a profit or even maximizing cash flow. There are growing numbers of people who barter because they prefer personal exchange over anonymous transactions, because they do not want to squander money and waste resources, because they can do without middlemen, because they like bargains, because they prefer to rely on themselves and those in their own community.

The most popular form of barter is the swap—a direct exchange between two people that is even in value.

We've all swapped for something, at least once or twice in our lives—because we needed it and a swap was the only way to get it, because the item was a luxury and we felt guilty about spending the money, because the occasion presented itself and we thought, why not?

Basically, we are no different from individuals who swap regularly, except they do it more often. They do it for convenience, for luxuries, for necessities they otherwise could not afford.

Valerie, for instance, lives in Los Angeles and does not drive. In Los Angeles that is highly inconvenient. But she works in film and she has access to screenings. She swaps her screening invitations for transportation, and manages to get around town very well.

Judy and Eddie Meyer swap mainly for luxuries. They are a middle-class, college-educated couple in their early forties. They have two children in college and they like comfort and lovely surroundings. Eddie had always been in the garment business, and seven years ago, in partnership with Judy, he started manufacturing chic chamois clothing. Soon they were selling expensive chamois bikinis, pants, skirts, and jackets to specialty shops all over the country. When their children left home for college, they decided there was no reason for them to endure Los Angeles smog anymore. They moved to Santa Cruz, into an old-fashioned bungalow in the middle of a small fruit orchard.

Generally, their swapping follows these principles:

1. **The swap is personal.** They only swap with people whose work they know, whom they like and respect.

2. **They swap for things with esthetic or luxury value.** They swap for Judy's handwoven clothes, Eddie's handmade clothes, their furniture, artistic decorations for the house, paintings, sculptures.

3. **They swap with friends for services.** They do not like selling chamois clothing to their friends, many of whom are professionals. Instead they give the clothes to them. This segues into barter arrangements for the services of lawyers, dentists, accountants.

4. **They use direct exchange.** They never get involved with third-party barter. They have heard of labor-credit systems and barter clubs, but they are not interested. If the premium were on efficiency, they would use money.

5. **Parity is essential.** It is important to them that the exchange be equal in value, but they try not to measure it in monetary equivalence. They prefer keeping the balance intuitive—"Does it feel right?"

6. **They let time lapse.** The exchange is not immediate. By allowing time to pass before repayment, they strengthen the bonds of the relationship and embue the process with a flow, a give and take.

7. **They reap tax advantages.** They do not record their loose, unstructured, friendly swaps.

Laura Swope, on the other hand, barters only for necessities. She lives with her husband, Thomas, a writer and a book salesman, and their two young children, in a house they own in Berkeley. Laura runs a child-care service to help supplement Thomas's precarious monthly income. Her swaps are organized along the following lines:

1. The swap is personal. She only swaps with parents of the children in her child-care center.

2. She swaps for necessities. Her attitude to barter is essentially practical. The parents of her charges have fixed floors, repaired ceilings, tuned her car, built play equipment, replaced old plumbing, and assisted her with the children.

3. She permits third-party barter. If a parent wants to bring someone else to do the barter, that is O.K. with Laura, as long as she does not get involved with the negotiations.

4. Parents determine parity. She asks them how many hours of child care they think the job is worth, accepts their estimate and leaves record keeping up to them. If she had to keep the records, she does not think barter would be worth it.

5. If the swap is never completed, the child is dropped from the day-care program. This has never happened.

Not all swappers are like Judy and Eddie or Laura. But everyone who swaps enjoys the notion of a personalized, direct transaction that avoids middlemen and taxes.

How do people go about accomplishing this personalized and mutually satisfying swap?

Although you can advertise in swap columns anywhere in the country, and pin up notices at supermarkets explaining what you have and what you want, the very best way to find out if someone will swap with you is to ask!

One woman had always paid her gynecologist in cash. When she and her husband separated, she had much less money to spend and, rather shyly, asked the doctor if he was interested in any of her ceramics. The doctor was delighted! He and his wife were gourmet cooks. They had been searching unsuccessfully for a set of special South American covered dishes. The woman could make them easily and pay her gynecological costs for a year.

A lawyer in Phoenix is always surprised that his clients with skills but little money do not suggest bartering. When he mentions that he is open to the idea, they are thrilled. The lawyer has a beautiful set of office bookshelves, a swimming pool that is cleaned regularly, and air conditioning in his house, all through swapping. The clients have saved considerable amounts of cash, and both parties enjoy a much closer, more satisfying lawyer-client relationship.

Whereas the horsetrader develops skills to edge out the other person in a deal, the swapper is more interested in determining whether the trade is equal. It is important for the swapper to determine parity ahead of time; that way neither party feels cheated.

But how do you determine parity? When artists trade with artists, or doctors with doctors, it is easy to assess equivalent values; the same criterion applies to each other's work. But how do plumbers and photographers work out their equivalent value, or jewelers and gardeners?

There are three ways to establish parity.

1. Judge the *market value*
2. Follow the general rule: *equal time = equal worth*
3. Trust your *intuitive response*

The obvious method of computation is to determine the regular market value of one's work and apply it directly to the trade. A photographer reports, for instance, that she and her plumber computed their services at standard rates. The plumber worked at $18 an hour, threw in parts for free and in return received a beautiful set of photos of his children that would otherwise have cost him $25. People feel comfortable with this method. The value of the barter is easy to see and conforms to everyday business experience.

Others, however, are inclined to value everyone's time and labor equally, regardless of the going market rate. There are two prevailing reasons for this. The first is need, the second is social philosophy.

When people barter out of need, the need becomes an equalizing force. Commodities or services, which under other circumstances might have quite disparate values, are equal in necessity and therefore rendered equal in value. When Martha, a midwife in Mendocino, California, needed firewood, she did not mind bartering her usual $150 fee for several cords which added up to less in market value. She was concentrating on keeping warm in the winter.

Then there are people whose social philosophy recognizes all labor as equal. What happens when you take an hour's worth of a psychiatrist's expertise and energy and compare it to an hour's worth of a carpenter's skill and energy? The psychiatrist normally receives a fee of $50 to $75 per hour; the carpenter, $8 to $15. Why is one hour of one person's time worth so much more than one hour of another's?

Ralph, a lawyer, is a product of Berkeley activism of the 1960s and has been involved with political communes and law collectives. He now owns a turn-of-the-century house, which he is restoring, near downtown Los Angeles. His nearby "walk-in" law office, featuring a sign made (for barter) by a local neon artist, services the Chicano community.

Ralph believes that all labor is equal in value. He especially feels that the value of legal services has been overinflated by social attitudes. For him, barter is a way to break down this conditioned way of thinking.

Last week, a Chicano wrought-iron worker came into his office. The man needed various settlement papers to be drawn. Ralph needed wrought-iron work done on his house. They swapped on an equal-labor-value basis. The man was pleased his work was so highly valued; Ralph felt he was getting a bargain since he could not do the wrought-iron work himself, nor was it something for which he would have paid cash.

Still others, like the Meyers in Santa Cruz, determine parity intuitively. They keep the swapping process fluid. A few months ago, for instance, Judy Meyer traded chamois clothes to have her portrait painted by an artist friend. When the portrait was completed, it turned out to be a major work in oil on a very large canvas and had taken a lot longer than the artist had anticipated. The Meyers felt that the original amount of clothes they had traded was inadequate payment for such a lot of work. So they gave the artist an open-ended credit in their shop. They like swaps to be flexible and spontaneous. Though a trade here and there might not be equal, they are getting what they want, what is meaningful to them, and, over the long run, they believe that everything balances out.

However, there is a danger in assessing the barter transaction on a predominantly intuitive basis: it is possible neither party will have a clear understanding of the other's expectations.

Sheila Kelly, a herbalist who lives just outside of Boulder, Colorado, traded mountain herbal walks in exchange for various offerings. She did not specify quantities nor a time period for the other person's barter to be completed. The results were unfortunate and she felt she had been cheated. After a while, she decided "vibes" weren't enough and began to state exactly what she expected in exchange for her services. Since that time, she has had no trouble. She gets her hand-knit sweater in time for winter, and her supply of freshly baked bread in plenty of time for dinner.

Surprisingly enough, very few people have complained of being cheated in their barter transactions. Their frustration usually arises from a job poorly done. Ralph, the lawyer who is restoring the old house, swapped legal work for a paint job. His client showed up drunk and painted wavy blue lines where straight white ones were supposed to go. But this was unusual. Ralph says that in general he has noticed a much stronger commitment to fulfill the barter payment than he has ever seen when cash was the only incentive for work done.

Many enthusiastic swappers get so carried away with the joy of swapping that they go overboard and forget to earn enough cash to cover their monthly expenses. When Charlie Alisio, an accountant in Taos, New Mexico, moved there from Brooklyn, he was so infatuated with his new life style that he swapped for everything. One day he looked around and realized he did not need two goats, or twelve egg-laying chickens, or more turquoise jewelry or leather vests. He needed more money to pay all his bills! Now he restricts his swapping to those items (such as parts and labor for a greenhouse) that he actually wants.

Swappers would do well to take the following tips:

1. Look for opportunities in swap columns, posted announcements, etc. But more important, if you want to swap for something, be direct. Ask!
2. Be explicit in stating your expectations.
3. Arrive at a mutual understanding in evaluating each other's goods and services.
4. If you want to barter more, spread the word. If you

want to barter less, or not with particular people, explain that you are low on cash.

5. Determine a balanced ratio between cash income and barter income.

6. Enjoy the bargain inherent in trading. It may take a little more time, but remember, you are not paying extra dollars in taxes or middlemen costs.

4.

Collective Barter

COMMUNITY BARTER

Statistics show that most Americans move at least once every five years. As a nation we are nostalgic for stable, continuous relationships—exemplified by television's Walton family—but we do not live in situations that foster them. Mobility takes its toll in the amount of trust with which we greet the frequent onslaught of new acquaintances. For our own emotional survival, we keep relationships superficial and object oriented. We have our work friends, our PTA associates, our golf and tennis chums. Rarely do we integrate all functions, all friends.

However, reappearing in the midst of this twentieth-century fragmentation are communities which do attempt to integrate these various categories. Some of them are "intentional," planned communities, based on a particular philosophy and adherence to a specified life style. Others are not planned. They consist of loose clusters of people with similar values, who behave toward each other with feelings of sharing and commitment.

Both types of communities practice barter. The intentional community often has a work-labor credit system that eliminates the necessity of money within the confines of the community. The loosely structured communities engage in reciprocity, mutual assistance, giving and receiving. The expectations and obligations involved in this reciprocity are not articulated.

Assistance means helping out—moving, yard work, household chores, repairs, transportation, child care, dinners, shopping, professional advice, tools, equipment. During a crisis, everyone who is part of the community shows support.

The people in these communities do not like the word barter. It makes their behavior look too much like quid pro quo. They prefer a word like neighborliness. But in fact, there is a definite feeling of obligation in these communities to do your part and an expectation that others will do their part for you. The big difference is that the guilt which is usually a part of the dynamics of extended families is absent. Though no ledgers are kept, "To refuse to give, like refusing to accept, is a refusal of friendship and intercourse."

Mountain Drive, California, is one of these caring, sharing communities. It is named after the road that climbs high in Los Padres Mountains above Santa Barbara. Tucked behind a row of mailboxes, off roads that veer sharp and steep into the folds of the hillside, it is a small, self-contained community of about a hundred people.

Originally populated by craftspeople and artisans, the bohemians of the 1950s, Mountain Drive was known for years as the birthplace of the hot tub. The houses all reflect the hand-built ethos which permeates this community. Recently, a sprinkling of professionals have moved in. But the general atmosphere here is that economic class is irrelevant; what counts today—as it did twenty years ago—is what you can do with your hands.

Sam is a potter. He crafted the walls of his home out of adobe, the ceilings with carved wood beams, and the floors with tiles of his own creation. Chickens poke around the patio. Nothing about the house is in a hurry. It fits in with the rhythm of the landscape—Indian, Spanish, Mexican, Californian.

Sam is about sixty years old, with a long shock of white

hair and a deep tan from working as a summer ranger in the Sierras. He explains that the undeveloped land originally was purchased by an unusual individual, Robert Hyde, who called himself "the futile baron." Hyde set a price of $50 down and chose his own settlers, "pioneering people," who could take care of themselves and build their own houses by hand. In exchange for the use of his bulldozer, cement mixer, and truck, they gave him portions of the olive oil and wine they produced. His bartering spirit remains after his death.

Sam describes the members of the community as a roving band of workers.

"I do for you. You do for me," is the way Sam puts it. "Last Sunday, for example, Tim invited me over for a pancake breakfast. 'By the way,' he said, 'The wind blew off my roof.' The next thing I knew, I was nailing down tar paper. On Monday, he came by with a truckload of firewood for me. So I gave him a jug of vinegar. That puts me one ahead!" Sam laughs.

Sam attributes the prevalence of bartering to the community's unique spirit, its talented members, and their lack of involvement with money per se. He remarks that they even have a market day once a month, when they exchange their goods with each other. The object is for no cash to change hands at all.

Moreover, people like Sam, who isolate themselves from the town, tend to rely on each other more. "Even the professionals feel it," he says. "There's a lawyer who lives here. She is irrevocably tied to this community. If we ever needed legal advice or assistance, she's help us out. We expect her to. If her house needs repair, she's expect us to help her. It's all based on trust."

The relative isolation of the community and the presence of persons with manual skills are key factors in many communities that practice barter.

Jerome, Arizona, for instance, is an old mining town taken over by craftspeople and artisans. Fifty-five percent of the people in Liberty Valley (the region which includes Jerome) have incomes that fall under the poverty level. In Jerome itself, located high up in the mountains, the rate of dollar turnover is only 1.1. The hordes of tourists who come each year to view the abandoned mine only spend 63¢ per car. Without barter, according to one Jerome shopkeeper, the people could not survive.

Labor, clothes, crafts, foodstuffs, meals in restaurants, and raw materials for crafts are all traded. Personal-service businesses do not exist in Jerome. Haircuts and shampoos are bartered. Even the homes are inhabited through barter. Deserted by their original owners when the ore vein ran out, they were taken over ten or fifteen years later by squatters. Eventually, these squatters—the present-day citizens of Jerome—looked up the title deeds and found the owners. They worked out deals in which they could either purchase or legally remain in the houses in exchange for renovating them.

A community similar in its isolation and economic needs is the Miccosukee Land Cooperative, ten miles out of Tallahassee, Florida. The land here has been purchased cooperatively; people come from all over the country and try to build their own homes.

Although eggs, milk, and vegetables are exchanged for other produce and for rides into town, the core of the bartering at Miccosukee centers around tools, construction skills, and child care. Most people spend their entire income on building their homes, and there is not a lot of extra money to go around. Lending other residents your tools insures that they will loan you theirs. Helping others with construction implies that they will help you in return. Because the community is without child care alternatives, trading baby-sitting time enables parents to have some time for themselves.

The bartering is neither philosophical nor organized. Howard Tilden, a journalist who lives on the land, asserts, "When you are dealing on a practical level, the way we are here—trying to get houses built—you organize on philosophical levels as little as possible." The barter is akin to favors. Money, feels Howard, is insulting among friends.

"If you use money to pay someone, the person who pays is in a superior position to the person who takes the money. It louses up the feeling of equality at the land coop."

Although community reciprocity seems easier in rural, isolated settings, it also exists within cities. In the Adams-Morgan community of Washington, D.C., in Carbondale, Illinois, in the French Quarter of New Orleans, in parts of Boston and in parts of the every major city, the presence of alternative businesses, tenant-rights organizations, food-distribution collectives, neighborhood gardens, and other neighborhood activist programs create an atmosphere which nurtures a great deal of nonstructured but highly visible reciprocity.

Echo Park, in Los Angeles, is an example of such an urban community. It is a high-density, heterogenous neighborhood with concentrated numbers of old houses and politically active people.

As in Mountain Drive, California, barter in Echo Park often takes the form of mutual assistance. When someone in the community has to move, for instance, everyone shows up and helps.

Jane, a radical carpenter, calls it the moving exchange. "It's a fact of the community. You help me move and I'll help you. It involves many people, twenty or so, to help one person move. And there's no guilt pressure, either. If you're busy, you're not required to be there. You do it because of commitment to each other, to the community."

The moving exchange has its equivalence in every other aspect of people's activities. There is an interdependency of all on the skills of the others, whether they are manual skills (repair, maintenance) or cerebral skills (medical or legal assistance).

Politics provides the cohesive glue for this particular community, playing a role not dissimilar to that of the church in nineteenth-century towns. The struggles to organize a food coop, a communal nursery school, law collectives, and United Farm Worker boycotts have united individuals in Echo Park into a group with common goals and shared values. But unlike a church, there is no minister, no institutional heirarchy here. Politics provides a base, but does not dictate a structure for social interaction.

Over two thousand years ago, Aristotle, in his *Politics*, contended that "to every kind of community (*koinonia*) there corresponds a kind of good will among its members which expresses itself in reciprocity."

Reciprocity implies feelings of mutuality, responsibility, and obligation. Mountain Drive, Jerome, Muccosukee Land Cooperative, and Echo Park are all examples of Aristotle's *koinonia*.

Jane speaks for everyone in these communities when she says, "I assume the people I know do not think of themselves as individual entities without external connections. I assume they are not relating to me on a purely business level. I feel we have something in common. I trust them. Therefore I can barter."

The key components of community barter include the following:

1. Need
2. Belief in the equality of people and their labor
3. Value of the personal over the impersonal
4. Common goals
5. Reluctance to mix friendship with money; lack of involvement with money
6. "Nonestablishment" life styles
7. Participation in community activities
8. Nonarticulated "expectation" and "obligation" shared by members of the community

BARTER CLUBS

Barter clubs, or trade exchanges, are membership organizations of business owners and professionals who trade with each other instead of paying cash. They are the newest wrinkle in the ancient history of barter; in essence, they are organizations through which people can barter without knowing each other or even ever meeting face to face.

Barter clubs first made their appearance in 1955 in California, when M. J. Hilton began to write his trading adventures in a little black notebook. He capitalized on his facility for matching need with finding product by including his friends and acquaintances. Finally, the little black notebook couldn't keep track of it all, so he set up an office and started Hilton Exchange. The climate in California was congenial. He survived, and the twenty-three-year-old Hilton Exchange is the longest-lived barter club in the country.

Other barter clubs evolved when lawyers, doctors, jewelers, and stationers, all friends, with long-standing business and social connections, decided that paying cash to each other was a waste of money. They could trade instead. These were small, friendly groups, operating out of garages, and using shoe boxes for files.

But from small beginnings, major trade clubs grew. In 1969, a combination of events occurred which soon catapulted barter clubs out of Southern California and sent them proliferating across the country. Inflation was the number-one event. Though the Nixon administration did not set wage and price controls until 1971, the business sections of newspapers across the land voiced mounting concern about inflation. Consumers did not have to read headlines to know that things were costing too much.

The other event was the availability of high-speed computers with memory banks. It took inveterate horsetraders with strong business backgrounds and active financial imaginations to seize the opportunity fostered by the dreary economic picture. Pouncing on the high-speed computers with memory banks, they figured out ways to expand the boundaries of trading. They created systems of cashless exchange, the modern-day barter clubs.

Barter clubs have exploded onto the 1970s economic scene. One old-time speculator gives barter clubs another three years before the sparks die out. However, many others predict that barter clubs not only will survive, but will live to see the demise of cash itself. Whatever their final fate, there is no doubt that at the present time, these clubs are going strong.

Their surge in popularity stems from an increased determination on the part of the middle class to hang onto its standard of living despite inflation and taxes. Barter clubs offer an answer. They are an organized way for people to get together and trade without the inconvenience of having to trade directly. The club functions as a *clearinghouse*, distributing information about what goods and services are available for trade; as a *bank*, keeping track of how much is earned or spent in trade; and as an *independent purchasing agent*, acquiring inventory for its members to obtain through trade.

By joining barter clubs, the average businessperson or professional has a chance to:

1. Conserve cash flow
2. Increase business
3. Convert perishable commodities into nonperishable commodities

4. Acquire an additional line of credit, which means more buying power

5. Trade for "life's little extras" without spending pocket money

6. Use a computerized bookkeeping system

7. Be guaranteed payment for goods or services delivered without collection problems

8. Trade wholesale to wholesale, thus garnering certain tax advantages

Barter clubs and their franchises can now be found all over the country. Business Exchange, one of the biggest (4,700 members and 27 franchises) is centered in Los Angeles. So is Mutual Credit Buying System (3,500 members), Hilton Exchange, and a host of smaller operations. Trade Americard (700 members) is located in Orange, California, and United Trade Club (1,600) in San José, California. The Executive Trade Club is in Honolulu; Exchange Enterprises (24 franchises) is in Salt Lake City, Utah, as are United Business Exchange and a few smaller clubs. Business Owners Exchange (350 members) is in Minneapolis, Minnesota; Charge-a-Trade and Barter Card are in Florida.

These clubs do a multimillion-dollar business in trade; Business Owners Exchange turned over a million dollars in 1976 alone. Both Mutual Credit Buying Systems and Business Exchange claim to have traded $12 million annually. These millions don't all come from the combined totals of each member's individual transaction. A club makes the leap from small time to big time when it starts dealing in media barter, due bills, real estate, insurance, and large bulk inventory. (Media barter is the exchange of available advertising time or space for manufacturers' products or due bills. Due bills are credits for hotel or restaurant rooms and meals.)

The barter club trades inventory (anything from land in the desert to Japanese steel or PSA plane tickets) for advertising time or space and then trades for more inventory. One club had land which it traded for a motel. It then traded a percentage of motel ownership with a billboard company for bus-bench advertising. A radio station traded air time for the advertising space on the bus bench. The club is now trading the air time for something else. A club will also pick up due bills from hotels or restaurants in exchange for printing costs or some other service it can provide. It then makes these due bills available to members, who use them for vacation or business purposes.

Franchises have helped turn barter clubs into big business. An active and aggressive sales policy insures not only new members but also new franchises all over the country. Some of them fold quickly, but many do not. The business climate in the country is receptive. Businesses will join today in places where they would not have joined ten years ago. They are ready to believe that when a barter-club operator says the club can save them money and increase their business, it really can.

How do these clubs operate? Standard procedure generally follows these lines:

1. Recruitment through friends and by salespeople
2. Initial joining fee (varies)
3. Use of vouchers, charge cards, checks, or scrip to record purchases made
4. Directory with names of members, goods, and services circulated in some clubs; others require calling the trade director
5. An 8 to 10 percent service fee charged on all transactions; sales tax paid by buyer in cash
6. Approval necessary on purchases over certain amounts; phone lines are kept open for this purpose
7. Newsletters sent to keep members abreast on newest members and the latest inventory bargains acquired by the club (due bills at a new hotel, fertilizer, or suntan lotion in large quantities from some member firm)
8. Members with large amounts of credit to spend are put on standby status—they do not "sell" goods or services in trade until they have spent their credit
9. Members are contacted and told about opportunities to buy land or insurance with trade
10. 50 percent memberships are available to businesses which need to keep their cash income above a certain amount for inventory purchases
11. Loans are issued at interest
12. Computer read-outs of members' credit-debit standings are sent out each month
13. Social get-togethers for members such as luncheons, dances, and junkets to Las Vegas occur on a regular basis

Though the barter clubs claim to be the first successful experiment in the creation of the cashless society, they did not invent indirect trade. Ancient Egypt, Sumeria, Babylonia, and Peru all had storage systems which revolved around centralized bookkeeping and a controlled redistribution process. Remember Joseph's interpretation of the Pharoah's dream? Seven years of plenty, seven years of famine. Wheat was collected from everywhere (in the form of a tax) and stored in central locations. It was then redistributed in time of need. Unlike their nomadic, direct-trading neighbors (Joseph's brothers, for instance), the Egyptians were able to survive the famine.

The computer keeps track of every barter club member's trade. It makes possible a pool of goods and services without the necessity of a huge warehouse in which to store everything. It is the modern technological version of those ancient storage systems.

Here is a diagram of the barter club as computerized storage unit, with the members as the indirect traders:

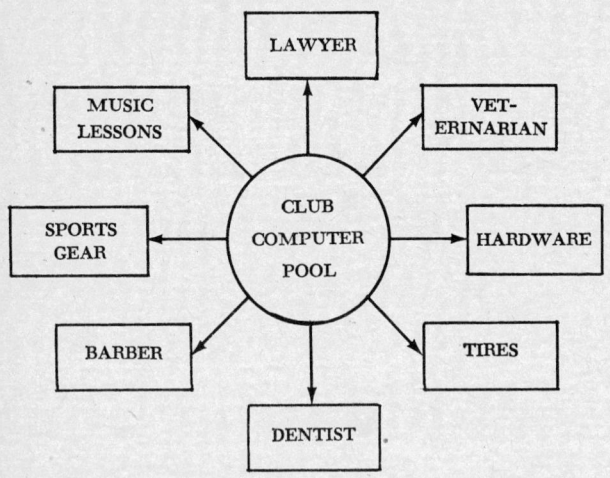

Now let us follow a trade.

1. X, who sells tires, has $100 worth of trade credit, accumulated by selling tires to members at full retail value. The wholesale cost of the tires was $50. X's profit was $50.

2. Y sells sports gear. X comes into Y's store. X purchases

$100 worth of gear, paying with club scrip. The sports gear cost Y $50, and so Y made a profit of $50.

3. $100 worth of trade credit is subtracted from X's account.

4. $100 worth of trade credit is added to Y's account.

5. Both X and Y made a wholesale to retail markup profit.

6. Y paid the 10 percent commission on the sale to the club.

7. Y then goes to Z, a music instructor, and arranges for a series of guitar lessons.

That is how it works on the simplest level. Very few members (and certainly not the management) keep things that simple.

When you walk into the offices of Mutual Credit Buying Systems (MCBS) in Los Angeles, past the rows of hustling salesmen making their pitches on the phone, past the long ribbons of computer read-outs, past doors labeled Jockey Club, Insurance, Real Estate, and into the glass rhomboid-shaped office of Tom Skala, MCBS's president, you realize that things can indeed get very complicated.

An MCBS membership directory lists thousands of names. A random page from the A section indicates the wide variety:

Accountants, Acoustical Ceilings, Acoustical Engineers, Acting Instruction, Actors, Acupuncturists, Adding & Calculating Machines, Advertising Services—Aerial, Agencies & Counselors, Art Services, Broadcasting, Catalog, Copy Writers, Direct Mail, Displays, Distribution Services, Motion Picture, Newspaper, Outdoor, Periodical, Photography, Radio, Schools; Air Cleaning & Purifying Equipment, Air Conditioning Contractors, Equipment, Air Travel—Ticket Agencies, Air Tube Systems, Aircraft Equipment, Aircraft Service & Maintenance, Aircraft Upholsters, Alarm Systems, Alteration Contractors, Alteration—Clothes, Animation, Answering Bureaus, Machines & Services, Antennas, Antique Brokers, Dealers, Restorers; Apartment Renting & Leasing, Apartments, Appliances, Major—Garbage Disposal Units, Ranges & Stoves, Sewing Machines, Television & Radio, Vacuum Cleaners, Washing Machines & Dryers, Appliances Small, Appliances Used,

Aquariums, Architects, Architect Supplies, Models, Art Dealers, Galleries, Art Goods, Art Objects—Packing & Shipping, Artificial Flowers & Plants, Artists, Commercial, Artists, Fine Arts, Asphalt, Astrologers, Audio Visual Equipment, Automobile—Repairing, Painting, Breaks, Dealers, Engine Exchanges, Leasing, Parts & Supplies, Road Service, Safety Certification, Upholstery, Service Stations, Services, Accessories, Air Conditioning Equipment, Body Customizing, Shock Absorbers, Stereophonic Equipment, Tires, Tops, Towing, Transmissions, Tune-ups, Unloading, Wrecking.

Besides giving the club members a wide variety for trade, the names under all these categories give the MCBS management, especially Tom Skala, the opportunity to wheel and deal in complex games involving any number of players.

Skala speaks of himself as a visionary, a financial seer. Seven years ago he created a program that was a form of computerized banking. Businesses didn't want it. "It was like future shock," says Skala. "No one believed a computer could take care of the credit and debit of the entire population; that an article could be paid for electronically with the push of a button by the time a customer left the store. If I had had a company then like Bank Americard, this barter club would be all over the country by now."

But though Skala talks about the cashless society in hypnotic tones and futuristic terms, his feet are planted firmly in the intricate business machinery of horsetrading. He remembers trades the way some people remember vacations, with complete itinerary and exact cost per item. His face lights up as he remembers, for instance, the time he parlayed a handful of used typewriters into a fortune in wigs by a baroque series of trades involving city lots, trust deeds, an old house, and finally the wigs, which he sold to a friend for forty thousand dollars.

He is more discreet about the real estate and insurance transactions he is working on at the moment, but he lets you know he has left wigs behind for much bigger and more profitable booty.

In this, Tom Skala is no different from any other head

of a barter club. No matter how many diplomas from business and law schools line the walls, no matter how many certificates in accounting, wherever there is a barter club, there is a horsetrader at the reins. Their freewheeling and triple-play dealing have found a profitable haven in the creation of these clubs. It is their time right now. Banking laws don't cover them. The IRS has yet to crack down.

M. J. McConnell, of Business Exchange, also in Los Angeles, is another example of a horsetrader in the respectable garb of a corporate president. When he was growing up during the Depression, he discovered that trading up was easier and more profitable than selling for cash. He traded a Model-T Ford to a tire dealer for four times what the original cost had been. He took the tires to a bottling company and traded them for soda pop in time to set up eleven stands for the Fourth of July soapbox derbies.

Now McConnell runs what is probably the most financially successful, least precarious, and, in the jargon of the business, among "the cleanest" of all the barter clubs. Business Exchange members range from individual small businesses to large wholesalers and manufacturers. But as you walk into his office, trip over the new shipment of American Indian jewelry and listen to him go through his moves on the phone, you realize that horsetrading is the name of the game and he loves to play it.

Most dues-paying members, however, do not share this passion for trading up. They pursue the object at hand and then bask in the bargain of it all. They feel no compulsion to parlay it into something else.

You can find two major personality types among the club's membership. The first type is content with simple trades. Usually recruited by persuasive salespeople, this type wants to see if the barter club can offer better deals, but has neither the time nor the inclination to put extra energy into it. This type gets discouraged easily and can become bitter if left with a lot of trade credit and no place to spend it.

The second personality type is the active member. Though not a horsetrader, this type "works" the club, often belonging to more than one barter club at a time. This type looks for the best deals, likes to negotiate and haggle, and sometimes even trades one club's scrip for another's. Belonging to barter clubs makes a big difference in this type's life. Such people rarely pay cash for anything.

John and Paula Winters are of this type.

John sells carpets. Paula works part-time in a delicatessen. They live in a modest middle-class neighborhood in West Los Angeles, where the lawns are green and all the children take lessons. The Winters have a twelve-year-old daughter and a nine-year-old son.

John and Paula are pragmatic about barter clubs. The clubs have their ups and downs. They believe trade credits should be strictly controlled because when they are not, mini-inflation hits the clubs and there is no value in belonging. However, even if there is no credit control, John and Paula have learned how to get what they want when they need it. They learned through experience. They joined their first club five years ago, and by the time they moved into their house a year later, they were able to have it painted inside and out, the yard landscaped, the plumbing fixed, the carpets cleaned and the wiring redone—all through trade!

They belong to three different barter clubs. The following schedule of their week indicates the extent to which they are able to integrate barter in their lives on a daily basis. And this schedule excludes the more unusual barter benefits, such as bartered vacations, car purchases, children's day camp, and parents' fiftieth wedding anniversary celebration.

MONDAY
Car repaired: both barter club and direct trade
Answering service: seven days a week, barter club
Cleaners: barter club
Fruit and vegetable shopping: barter club, 50 percent cash, 50 percent trade ,
Paula goes to gym: barter club

TUESDAY
Paula gets prescription glasses: barter club (doctor and dental/medical services are on direct trade)
John goes to health club: barter club

WEDNESDAY
Tennis lessons for two children: barter club (tennis clothes and shoes also through barter club)

Pet needs—fish, aquarium, puppy, puppy food: barter club

John buys shoes: barter club

THURSDAY

Gardener: barter club

Plumber and electrician for repairs: direct trade

Lamp fixed: barter club

Paula sews daughter's skirt: sewing machine through barter club

FRIDAY

Music lessons for children: barter club

Dinner in restaurant: barter club

SATURDAY

Ballet and tap-dance lessons for daughter: barter club

Haircut for John: barter club

Car washed: barter club

Dinner in restaurant: barter club

Movies: three-way deal (John did a carpet job for movie passes)

SUNDAY

T.V. and eight-track stereo: barter club

Carpenter: moonlights on barter club

Trade fair: sponsored by barter clubs; people display merchandise to buy with credit. They buy son a bike, and get new pots for the kitchen.

The Winters have an unabashed love of possessions and a total disinclination to pay cash for them. But they are quick to point out that it's not worth running all over town for a three- or four-dollar item, even if you could get it for trade.

Nonetheless, it can be very gratifying to accomplish something entirely by trade, even if it does mean putting out a little extra work. Jerry Binder, public relations person for MCBS, illustrates this fact with the story of a wedding.

An MCBS employee and his bride-to-be went to Las Vegas to be married. Their wedding rings came from a member jeweler, through barter. They were put up at the Jockey Club in Las Vegas, through barter. The wedding took place at the Silver Bell Chapel; the minister performed the services, the chapel supplied photographers, corsage, and tape recording, the wedding party ate dinner at Gus Gallo's—all through barter. With a due bill that MCBS had purchased and given them on barter, the happy wedding couple, their family, and friends all saw a show at the Tropicana.

As for Jerry himself, "I only use cash," he says, "for tips and taxes."

The following are helpful tips for barter club members:

1. Belonging to a barter club means trading now for something you will want in the future. Know what you want and go after it as soon as it is available, otherwise it will disappear and you'll be out of luck. Be aggressive.
2. On the other hand, be patient. Don't give up the minute you can't get what you want.
3. Don't accumulate too much credit.
4. Don't borrow a lot of credit from the club. They charge high interest rates.
5. Remember not to go overboard. Though it does not feel like money, it is still costing you. You are not getting things for free.
6. Feel free to call the trade director and voice complaints, suggestions. Get to know the people who run the club. That way you will be informed about new members and the latest deals in inventory before the rest of the membership has traded them dry.
7. Check your computer read-outs closely. Sometimes there are errors in the club's favor.
8. Take advantage of trades even when you don't need the items at the moment; they will be useful later on.
9. Report people who try to cheat you or who renege on a deal to club management.
10. Maximize your energy. Don't waste it on tracking down trades that are not worth the effort.

NETWORKS AND EXCHANGES

Like community barter, networks and exchanges are nonprofit and egalitarian. There are times, however, when the give and take of community barter needs to be more structured. There are times when the need for personal connection propels the individual barterer into formalizing the hit-or-miss nature of the swap process. This is when networks and exchanges come in handy.

Networks are a lateral form of organizing persons and groups. The bartering in networks usually centers around intangibles—information, the energy for coordinating political, psychological, or spiritual activity, and for maintaining coalitions. Networks aim for the equal distribution of responsibility, power, and effect without the gross inefficiency which sometimes accompanies leaderless efforts. The key word is *link*. Networks provide links where the exchange of information and social effort can transpire. These links give coherency along with flexibility.

Anne Dosher, of San Diego's Community Congress Network, states that unlike traditional forms of organization with one power focus, "network power is distributed in interconnected, horizontal paths which provide a tougher, more resilient, enduring system, well suited to the long-term task of altering existing social and political institutions and values."

Exchanges, on the other hand, are centrally organized and revolve around the bartering of tangible goods and services. Sometimes they serve a particular purpose. There are learning exchanges, vacation exchanges, transportation exchanges. But the majority of exchanges, like barter clubs, are all-purpose.

They list goods and services, and they record labor done and labor received. Contact between members is funneled through a central office. Unlike networks, exchanges do not rely on the participants' drawing their own lines of connection. However, they do share the same nonprofit orientation and the aim of changing socioeconomic patterns.

It is not accidental that networks and exchanges have developed in the 1970s. The energy of movement politics of the 1960s has been dissipated. Government palliatives, such as OEO, have been eliminated. Hippies are no longer leading the media in antimaterialist consciousness. They are, as the manager of Switchboard, an alternative information center, put it, "poor people, just like poor people everywhere."

It was time for new systems of organization and communication.

Networks and exchanges do not appear to be revolutionary. Bank of America buildings have been left intact and SWAT forces have yet to smash the computers which give the people access to information.

Nonetheless, organizers of networks and exchanges realize they are assaulting not property, but the system upon which property is unfairly accumulated. They see networks and exchanges as a counterforce against centralized, profit-oriented systems, such as banks and corporations, which, by their very nature, are secretive and competitive.

The bartering of information and ideas is an essential ingredient in the network-exchange construct. In the United States, we hoard expertise. We sell it only to the "right" customer. It is as radical to suggest that ideas and research information should be available to all as it is to suggest that private property be abolished.

Exchanges and networks postulate that only through free access to information will we be able to affect the political and economic processes which structure our lives.

The Conference for Economic Democracy, a coalition organized by Tom Hayden and other activists in California, has integrated an information-sharing network into its program in order to facilitate political actions across the state. Community Market, a group in Louisa, Virginia, uses its producer-consumer catalogue of "countereconomy" information as a vehicle to enable people across the country to contact each other and ultimately to "replace capitalism with a democratic, decentralized economic system."

Berkeley and San Francisco are communities gridded by networks. These interconnect consumer coops, food distribution centers, "new-age entrepreneurs," and radical collectives ranging from auto-mechanics collectives to answering-service collectives. By giving people access to information and ensuring mutual support, the networks create a nonhierarchical power base that proves it is possible to have a system of organization that survives by sharing, that does not alienate workers from product, consumers from process, and people from people.

How do these networks work?

A questionnaire is sent to as many people and organizations relevant to the network as possible. The information is collated by a central coordinating committee (composed of individuals most dedicated to getting the network going). The information then is put into computers, directories, or files and made available to anyone belonging to the network.

Questions vary with the network's focus. Pertinent information for networks organized around people interested in group marriages or other forms of group living would be different from information for alternative businesses. The questionnaire from Self/Determination, a personal/political network organized by John Vasconcellos, a California assemblyman, inquires about a person's field, which may or may not mean job—"it is the concept on which you are activating . . . a social, political, or personal cause"; about skills— "what you do best"; about fantasy or vision—"the creative spark for action."

The Conference for Economic Democracy has gathered data about who has expertise in what field, from child care to military analysis; who would work for what cause and by what method. For instance, if you are a member of CED and you are involved with a save-the-whales campaign, you would call and find out the names of conservationists, ecologists, and fishing-industry experts in all parts of your state. You would contact them yourself and use their skills in organizing a state-wide action. In return, they would expect your cooperation for their programs.

Exchanges are barter clubs with a difference. They function as an information clearinghouse and as a mini–energy bank, recording work done and work received. They offer a wide variety of goods and services and instruction. They do not exist to make a profit.

The Community Energy Bank in Eugene, Oregon, for example, includes all aspects of agriculture (from animal husbandry to irrigation systems), arts and crafts, business, finance and real estate, construction skills and supplies, domestic skills, entertainment, health (including acupressure, massage, and midwifery), humanities, social sciences, education, spiritual awareness, sports, games, transportation, and a host of other categories.

Although members of exchanges often pay dues, the amount is small. Commissions are not charged on trade transactions. Accumulation of real estate and other inventory for profitable trade does not take place. Moreover, in the words of Community Energy Bank's contact person, Candy Moffat, the exchange is formed as a "constructive alternative to the 'money talks' power structure," not, as with barter clubs, to increase business and preserve cash flow.

Exchanges are often organized to help people help themselves. Barter is not a panacea for all social ills, but the use of direct, concrete exchange gives people a sense of control over their economic destiny. This is significant for those groups divested of that control—the unemployed, those on welfare, teenagers, and the elderly.

In Salt Lake City, Dorothy Pulley, of the People's Freeway Community Center (named because it turned freeway access land into vegetable gardens), relates how the center originally started as a neighborhood council in the heart of the city and then took over the poverty program. "We learned how to turn our welfare recipients, consumers, into providers." One of the ways in which that happened was through labor exchange. "There are so many low-income people with so many needs. They are best helped by the people who have the same problems."

She is joined in this belief by a volunteer social service agency in Carbondale, Illinois, which is gathering skills and experience information among the desperately poor and unemployed in the surrounding counties. The agency hopes to get an exchange started which will ease the financial situation for this poverty-struck area.

The Gray Bears, a senior-citizen organization in Santa Cruz, has formed a service exchange so that the elderly will not have to spend precious dollars for household repairs.

And in Portland, Oregon, a few years ago, during a peak period of unemployment, Wayne Mayo sat listening to his minister preach.

"Jesus told his disciples they were the salt of the earth." Inspired by these words, plus the bleak economic picture in Portland, Wayne and his friends decided that salt was used for preserving, for making things last longer, and maybe they could do that for people's money. They started the Service Exchange.

The Service Exchange now has 13,000 to 15,000 members, most of whom are unemployed. It does not use a credit-debit system (as does Community Energy Bank) because it feels that with so large a membership, contact would be too cumbersome and impersonal. Instead, a three-way phone system puts people in touch with each other, with the third party a Service Exchange worker.

Says Mayo, "I thought people might be afraid to call each other directly. We call first and take the stigma away. We prepare people for negotiating with each other. Very few people know how to barter. Once they get started in the exchange, they do it on their own. That's great! When something like barter is available when you're unemployed, it's an alternative to stealing!"

How do exchanges keep track of labor done and received?

The Service Exchange phones to see if everything is all right. Community Energy Bank relies on the members to report their own hours, given or taken in "energy." If members accumulate twenty hours or more in debts, they are flagged and asked to reduce the amount by contributing energy. If they accumulate large credits, they are flagged and asked to use some up.

The honor system seems to work. Members of Community Energy Bank report their hours. In Los Angeles, Free SIG (Special Interests Group), a Mensa-sponsored labor coop, goes even further. It requires no accounting of time put in or taken out. It trusts its 150 members to keep track of their own labor. If members are unable to respond to a work call within a week, they officially go on "overload" until their schedule lightens up.

Do people cheat by first using the exchange to get work done, and then never fulfilling their obligation? So far, this does not seem to be a problem. Perhaps Free SIG's stringent membership-application form screens out potential do-nothings, perhaps the system of double reporting (by the doer and taker) used by the Community Energy Bank constitutes an adequate check.

However, exchanges, like networks, and unlike barter clubs, are based on trust. In networks, there is a moral commitment to reciprocate in the areas and by the methods the member has indicated for information and aid in areas the member requests. In exchanges, there is the expectation that the member will work when called upon—otherwise why would that member have joined? The vision of humanity is an optimistic one. People are trustworthy, caring, and responsible, especially when they are treated that way.

There are times and places, such as now in parts of the Northwest, and in the San Francisco Bay area, when networks and exchanges coalesce. Bartering for goods and services remains local and specific. Networks, comprised in part of the bartering groups, spread over a wide geographic area and create a method for linking these groups. They give the horizontal superstructure which not only facilitates communication, but spreads power evenly. A diagram of such programs looks like this:

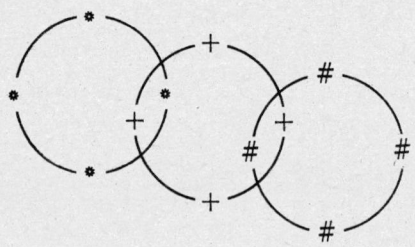

❋ GOODS AND SKILLS EX-   # CORE ACTION GROUPS,
   CHANGE   TRANSPORTATION UNITS
+ INFORMATION CENTERS

When networks and exchanges function together, the outlines of a social reorganization appear. It is possible to see at least sections of our society working smoothly in a nonprofit system based on equality, reciprocity, and trust.

The following advice is useful in deciding whether to participate in networks and exchanges:

1. Don't join unless you mean to participate.
2. Do not commercialize exchange relationships—don't ask if the person for whom you are doing the yard work wants to hire you on a weekly basis. (If the person brings it up, that's fine.)
3. Be honest about your skills and expertise. If you exaggerate your ability, you are only creating opportunities for complaints, criticism, and the eventual dismantling of the exchange or network.

4. This is not a business. If you have criticisms, shoulder some of the responsibility, and help make things better.
5. Take advantage of the personal nature of the organizations—make friends, verbalize feelings, participate in the unexpected. If you've never had a massage or folk-dancing lessons, try it. It's not costing a penny!

5.

The Economics of Barter

For at least another hundred years
we must pretend to ourselves that
fair is foul and foul is fair; for
foul is useful and fair is not.
Avarice and usury and precaution must
be our gods for a little longer still.   —LORD KEYNES

BARTER AS DECENTRALIST ECONOMICS

About 1860, as Darwin was developing his theories of survival of the fittest, a Russian military surveyor and natural scientist, Peter Kropotkin, later known as the Anarchist Prince, was making observations in Siberia that would eventually result in a theory of survival based on cooperation and mutual assistance.

Kropotkin wrote, "There is no infamy in civilized society . . . which would not have found its excuse in [Darwin's] formula of the survival of the fittest." Kropotkin's own view was that the element of struggle common to every species was directed not in competition against its own kind, but "against all natural conditions unfavorable to the species." Those who did not cooperate were "doomed to decay."

Kropotkin's theory of mutual aid not only suggested that people living in small local units would help each other and successfully manage to govern themselves without state interference, but that an ideal economy was one of self-sufficiency on a local, decentralized, and democratic level. Moreover, he maintained that the means of production, both agricultural and industrial, should be integrated and balanced with all other aspects of life. Barter, a nonmonetary and nonprofit form of exchange, was part of this natural and ideal order.

The nineteenth century, however, was much more inclined to embrace Darwin's view of survival of the fittest, allowing it to become a quasi-religious "scientific" justification of an unregulated market system and a rampant materialism. Heedless of the fact that the fiber of society was unraveling, more and more people embraced the Industrial Revolution and its institutional consequences. Economic theories that espoused the small, local, or human were deemed "utopian," impractical, and unnecessary. As economic historian Karl Polanyi puts it, "The new creed was utterly materialistic and believed that all human problems could be resolved given an unlimited amount of material commodities."

Today, we have ceased to believe that unlimited material commodities can solve all human problems. Our faith in a self-regulatory market system vanished long ago. Our confidence in central planning by lumbering bureaucracies is shaky, to say the least. We question policies of growth and expansion. We see land and resources devoured, mental health jeopardized, and we worry about the ravages of materialism. Not convinced that state socialism is any better a solution to contemporary problems than state capitalism, we are attracted to those humanistic theories that distrust centralized power and mass thinking and were deemed impractical a hundred years ago.

At first, the notion of decentralized economics remained improbable and romantic, part of the 1960s youth ideology. But gradually the idea has become more and more acceptable —decentralize, cut back, form small, manageable social units. Let control emanate from the people directly involved.

Kropotkin's theories are again popular. Our social critics refer to him. His brand of anarchism no longer conjures images of mad bomb throwers, but suggests a possible prototype for the organization of small groups of people into communities. We respond to his integration of rural and urban experience. We share his predilection for local control and nonhierarchical planning. We experiment with working communally. We too begin to see clearly the interdependence of all things on each other, and we return to his theory of mutual aid in an effort to learn how not to exploit.

Like Kropotkin, we have begun to appreciate that economic relationships concern more than competition and monetary gain. We seek ways to make these relationships nonexploitative and realize, as he did, that the direct equal exchange of goods and labor helps to eliminate exploitation, waste, and the concentration of power. The beauty of barter is that it can function in a democratic society without causing violent upheavals, and yet it helps transform oppressive nineteenth-century economic attitudes to be more responsive to our real contemporary needs.

The economist Kenneth Boulding, in his book *Beyond Economics*, explores moral issues ignored by Keynesian theory and by the preoccupation with massive production and consumption. He talks about "the economics of the coming Spaceship Earth." Unlike the open, expansive "cowboy economy" in which consumption was regarded as a good thing, we must now adjust to "spaceman economy," in which "through-put" is "something to be minimized rather than maximized. The essential measure of the success of the economy is not production and consumption at all, but the nature, extent, quality, and complexity of the total capital stock, including in this the state of the human bodies and minds included in the system." He adds that the idea of production and consumption as negatives "is very strange to economists who have been obsessed with income-flow concepts to the exclusion, almost, of capital-stock concepts."

Another economist currently enjoying tremendous popularity, E. F. Schumacher, shares Boulding's concern. On his recent tour through the United States (just before his death), Schumacher lectured to auditoriums overflowing not with "back to the landers" or communards, but with government officials and members of the business community.

His book *Small is Beautiful* espouses a philosophy of

"economics as if people mattered." Integral to this thinking is the notion that we must develop an intermediate technology which makes simpler and cheaper methods and equipment for production available to everyone and that are suitable for small-scale application compatible with a human need for creativity. He calls for a redressing of ecological imbalance and an end to "giantism" and "megapolism"—people matter more in small units than they do in large ones.

Schumacher has some anarchistic strains; indeed, he advocates many of Kropotkin's principles. As Theodore Roszak writes in the introduction to Schumacher's book, "Bigness is the nemesis of anarchism, whether the bigness is that of public or private bureaucracies, because from bigness comes impersonality, insensitivity, and a lust to concentrate abstract power."

Bigness is attacked by limiting the scale of technology, creating decentralized units of control, and addressing the issue of need rather than greed.

Many who were affected by movement politics or the general moral climate of the 1960s face a curious dilemma. Now that they've turned thirty, and settled down to a more conventional existence, how do they preserve the values they fought for a decade ago? They don't see themselves grabbing what they can get from the establishment while simultaneously working actively for its demise. They see the importance of the quality of life as they live it daily, regardless of their long-term political goals.

For this reason, the decentralist economics of "smallness" and the anarchist model of federations ("affinity groups") linked laterally in a nonauthoritarian manner provide an appealing present-day alternative. By creating networks out of affinity groups (such as neighborhood organizations, work collectives, food-distribution systems, people-owned small-scale factories, child-care programs, community gardens, clinics, alternative businesses, schools, local credit unions, and banks), they can reduce those aspects of society they consider exploitative and augment those they consider beneficial. While coexisting uneasily with established corporate and big-government institutions, they can start poking at the chinks in those institutions.

BARTER AS A MEANS

What role does barter play in all this?

Nobody claims that only through barter will society reach the blessed state of Schumacher's economics. Nor will barter be the tool to dismember capitalism single-handedly. But in its own modest way, barter can contribute to a reorganization of economic behavior that, while it is firmly planted in democratic tradition, reflects the best and most practical in anarchist thought.

The reason for this lies in the integrative aspects of barter. People who barter speak about it in the context of relationships, community, self-sufficiency, the worth of their own labor and their respect for the labor of others. They speak of the balance between independence from corporate superstructures and governmental patronization, and mutual support based on cooperative, noncompetitive economic relationships with others. Kropotkin, were he alive today, would applaud the sentiments of those barterers who use direct and indirect exchange as a way of transforming the nature of economic relationships into something other than monetary gain.

Because barter takes exchange out of a large, abstract, and centralized commercial superstructure and places it in an intimate, personal environment, it has useful application in decentralized "spaceman" economics.

When economic transactions take place on a person-to-person basis, feelings of responsibility, honesty, even caring often accompany them. A businessperson who doesn't know the customer is not necessarily concerned about selling inferior goods. And though some barterers are horsetraders, even they do not rationalize their behavior with defensive palaver about "good business practices."

In a startling book about consumer debt in America, *Consumers in Trouble*, David Caplovitz points out that when debtors who know their creditors default, they rarely are sued. The debtor is able to explain the default, and the creditor makes an appropriate adjustment. However, most consumer-debtors do not know their creditors. When they default, they are sued instantly. The suit is almost always successful, even when such extenuating circumstances as deceptive practices by the creditor indicate otherwise.

A solution has been proposed: neighborhood courts. The creditor would have to bring legal action into the neighborhood in which the debtor lives. This takes the process out of a formal structure and places it into a personal, local one. Caplovitz says that research has proven that when people have the opportunity for face-to-fact communication, they tend to work out accommodations.

Bartering, though directly tied in with the love of (or need for) possession, also frees the barterer from possessiveness. There is less hoarding and more willingness to part with objects. There is also little inclination to overproduce.

You begin to practice "spaceman economy." Ecosystems are not annihilated in an effort to maximize production. Nothing is gained by having a surplus. You exchange what you have for what you need or want, but do not secrete special "bartering accounts" the way you do with money, stocks, bonds, and other paper investments. This is because barter is concrete. You can see what you have. Enough is enough.

Moreover, because of its enormous flexibility, barter can be a link between one decentralized unit and the next. The extent of interconnection can remain limited or it can grow laterally, forming a pliable and resilient structure for interconnection. Small affinity groups, separate and unconnected to each other, do not comprise a system of any sort. The exchange of goods, services, and information is a crucial means of strengthening the bonds of community which connect one group to the next.

Barter may not effect change in our society's overall relationship to the market system—something that won't happen until the means of production undergo radical transformation. But for those individuals and small groups which practice barter, it serves to keep alive the hope that someday we will live in what Martin Buber calls "an organic commonwealth," that is, "a community of communities."

BARTER AS GUERRILLA ECONOMICS

Barter encompasses mutuality and connectedness, helping reinforce our communitarian impulses through social exchange. But it is also a form of individual guerrilla economics, spearheading autonomous attacks on middlemen, taxes, and the corporate squeeze.

Do not underestimate the power of the swap! It possesses all the advantages of traditional guerrilla tactics. It does not require large troops; it is flexible, hard to pin down, and once it's gone, it leaves no trace. It does not depend on fancy offices, elaborate equipment, or rigid schedules. It works as well in the city as it does in the woods.

Moreover, it has been a favorite tactic of people in times of economic adversity. During the 1930s, barter groups sprang up spontaneously all over the country as a survival technique for fighting the Depression. When Upton Sinclair, motivated by a desire to change the economic situation and to create a new and just society, ran for governor of California during this period, he pointed out the dramatic success of these spontaneous barter groups. He incorporated their principles in a campaign platform that advocated cooperatively owned factories, land colonies, homes possessed through barter, and labor value remunerated in scrip. In his EPIC (End Poverty in California) pamphlet, he wrote:

> I visited one of these groups in Pomona. In an old garage they had set up half a dozen rickety oil stoves, each with a wash boiler on top. With this primitive equipment they had stacked up half the garage with crates of canned peaches and tomatoes. When I offered to buy some of these goods, I was told that they were not permitted to be sold.
>
> I visited the UXA, a large barter group in Oakland, and listened to curious tales of how they had managed to drum up business for themselves. They would find a crop of fruit which the farmer would let them have, in return for painting his barn; they would find a paint merchant who would take a cord of wood from a man who would take some of the fruit. Some of the deals were highly involved with dozens of different services in a circle of transactions. . . .
>
> I assert that these self-help and barter groups represent Americanism more truly than any other phenomenon of our time. They embody all our true pioneer virtues—self-reliance, initiative, frugality, equality, neighborliness. They are the most precious product of the depression; and what have we done with them? The answer is that

we have done everything to handicap them, to humiliate them, to buy their leaders away from them. Why? Partly because they are believed to threaten "big business," but mainly because they threaten the "relief racket" which has become the mainstay of the politicians in these difficult times.

Sinclair rightly linked big business to massive government aid. He fought against the aid because he felt only by changing the economic system and putting it in the hands of the people would there ever be a chance for a viable and just society. He had a full grasp of barter's revolutionary power.

Barter in the 1930s was a guerrilla tactic, adopted by disenfranchised people—broke, unemployed, and stubborn—who proved they could survive economic adversity and create a new system that thumbed its nose at big business and at the debilitating effects of relief.

Barter still functions as a guerrilla tactic, even though we are not in the midst of a great depression. First, *it eliminates corporate overhead*. If you are a barterer, you do not need Madison Avenue or market research analysts or eye-catching packaging to dictate what commodity to buy. You know your own mind. You are able to circumvent consumer totalitarianism by going directly for what you are after and working out your own deal. If you want an orange, and an orange tree grows down the street, you can kiss Sunkist, and the extra you would pay in overhead, good-bye.

Second, *barter gets rid of middlemen*. Middlemen demoralize people into believing they are helpless. That way middlemen remain necessary and force people to put up with the inflation they produce. It is amazing how their absence lowers costs and increases everyone's feeling of self-sufficiency.

During the 1930s, Ralph Borsodi, a highly respected heretical economist (he is now ninety years old and still active), wrote about the incredible waste caused by the excessive middleman phenomenon. He maintained that actual manufacturing costs were only a small percentage of total costs. The rest was due to the elaborate, unnecessary costs of large-scale production and distribution. Railroad men, wholesalers, retailers, brokers, accountants, and clerks stood between the consumers and the goods they purchased. "Had we devoted some of the increase in technical knowledge . . . to small-scale production," he wrote, "there is not the slightest doubt that we would have raised the plane of living more than we have actually done."

Third, *barter punctures the abstract and illusory power of money*. Money is a metaphor. Presumably, it is a convenient metaphor for the real value of something, somewhere. It used to be that a paper dollar was redeemable in silver. No longer. A paper dollar is redeemable only for what an arbitrary combination of Dow Jones averages, the government, corporate decisions, and the local business climate say it is. The dollar inflates and deflates without logic, and yet it has immense power over peoples' lives.

Borsodi recently conducted an experiment in Exeter, New Hampshire. He convinced the citizens and the banks to cooperate in a commodity-backed currency that would not depreciate because it was based on genuine commodities. The banks issued scrip backed by "copper, tin, wheat, petroleum, and a host of other commodities, including, yes, even peanuts!" If people wanted to redeem the scrip, they could. Once he illustrated that an inflation-proof system could exist, particularly if the government were left out of the printing of currency and the arbitrary control of its value, Borsodi ended the experiment.

In his experiment Borsodi essentially went back to a version of beaverskin tokens. Using barter items, concrete and real, he took the mystique out of government-issued dollars and showed that people and local institutions could be trusted to regulate their own economic situation.

Experiments like Borsodi's are possible, but rarely happen without someone to organize them. Ironically, barter on an organized level is practiced by those institutions which stand in the way of barter on an individual level—corporations and government.

Such institutions appreciate barter's power to free them from certain tax obligations and allow them to work more advantageously within restrictive tariff systems. On the theory that we can always learn from the opposition, let us examine how some of these institutions work their exchanges.

BARTER AS BIG BUSINESS

1. Nations. *The Wall Street Journal* (1-12-77) reports that "Iran will try to switch to a barter system in its direct petroleum sales. It will swap its oil for commodities, a method that Iran currently uses with the Soviet bloc countries."

The United States has traded cotton, rye, tobacco, rice, wheat, barley, corn and grain sorghums for strategic materials, goods, or equipment required in connection with foreign economic and military aid, such as aluminum, asbestos, bauxite, manganese ore, and tin. Barter is described as a "useful device for getting around trading difficulties arising from currency regulations and trade barriers." According to Robert L. Rudy, deputy director of the Export Sales Division of the U.S. Department of Agriculture, "Between 1950 and 1967, approximately sixty strategic materials having a value exceeding $12 billion from over fifty different countries, and agricultural commodities having approximately the same dollar value, were exported to virtually every foreign country." The program was discontinued in 1973, possibly because of the Canadian-American grain lobby, which pointed out that "*it is precisely this flexibility which gives the barter program a potential for interference in normal commercial markets.*" What they mean by interference is manipulation of the "free market" by government price fixing, essentially interference with their profits.

2. Corporations. There are three kinds of corporate barter. First, there are times when corporations barter because raw materials are scarce, or because they would like the raw materials to appear scarce. The hefty amount of barter by chemical and oil companies falls into this category. In this context, James T. Halverson, director of the Federal Trade Commission's Bureau of Competition, has said, "We are particularly concerned about the survival of small, nonintegrated firms whose sources of supply have been cut off." The big companies, through barter, have manipulated the availability of supplies, beguiled the public into thinking supplies were scarce, and so justified unfair price increases.

Second, on international levels, more and more American corporations are bartering with third-world countries whose currency reserves are slim. According to *The Wall Street Journal* (5-18-77), "U.S. salesmen who are trying to win foreign customers to jet aircraft or similar big-ticket items often find they must think in terms of accepting olive oil or clothing to land a sale."

Corporations engage in a third type of barter as well—mergers. When a merger occurs, stock from company A is given to stockholders in company B, and vice versa. Although enormous profit might have been made in this exchange, *tax on the profit, though not foregone, is delayed until such time as the holders wish to sell out.*

3. Media. Station time not used is time wasted. Therefore, stations are always willing to take noncash customers on a best-time-available basis. How does it work?

An advertiser comes into a station which features give-away contests. It says, "I have $5,000-worth of top name-brand cosmetic products (worth $2,000 wholesale) for you to give away on your show in exchange for advertising time." The station needs to get rid of its unsold time and makes the deal.

It must declare the goods as value received, *but shows the value as lower than wholesale cost—FOB (Fee on Board).* The price is deflated to where it would be if the product were still in the warehouse.

Moreover, stations are often not paid in product, but receive payment in due bills, airline tickets, or restaurant credit. When this happens, the value received is then charged off as expense—salespeople take clients to restaurants, board meetings are held at hotels—and no tax need be paid. This is called a *tax wash.*

4. Traders. Seizing upon Part 111 of the tax code—*common, nontaxable exchanges*—real estate speculators, are collectors, coin and gun dealers, machinery and equipment investors all manage to make enormous profit by *bartering like for like,* therefore avoiding taxes until the time it is opportune for them to "cash out."

5. Barter barons. Some people, like William Tanner or Moreton Binn, head barter houses that specialize in media trades, whereby advertising time or space on television or radio or in magazines is exchanged for hotel space, equipment, and other commodities. Binn's company, Atwood Richards, has expanded to include everything from jet aircraft to bat manure. According to a report in the *Los Angeles Times,* it uses its $11 million media inventory to acquire such diverse products as toys, carpeting, and contraceptives. Its average trade is valued at $300,000, with none less than $50,000. Atwood Richards's biggest trade to date involved unloading $6 million worth of insecticide. According to Binn, the three things barter does for a business are increase cash flow, provide new business, and move excess inventory out that would normally be disposed of at close-out prices.

Presumably, the IRS does not consider this kind of barter "personal favors among friends." However, the elaborate negotiations involved in buying faltering business close-outs, or defective thermometers, or the unused capacity of a plant's production gives someone like Binn flexibility in the calculations of business losses and expenses.

There are other types of barter barons, those who barter volumes of business on the international scene. Most of them are to be found in Europe, where they live like Renaissance princes. *Forbes* magazine reports that they are rulers unto themselves, without national loyalty. Refugees from one place or another, they create their own fiefdoms through barter. Hungarian-born Simon Moskovics, for example, is known as "The King of the Switchers." Much in the manner of *Catch-22*'s Milo Minderbinder, he will acquire one product from one country, such as Egyptian cotton, and unload it at great profit in another. Fellow barter baron, Hendricks, lives in the style of a Hapsburg nobleman in present-day Germany, grossing between $7 and $8 million a year in barter transactions. Through timely manipulations of local economies on an international scale, these people manage to avoid paying too much into the tax coffers of any one counrty.

One of the most impressive of the barter barons is an American, Dr. Armand Hammer. At the age of twenty-three, he went to Russia to collect on debts owed to his family's pharmaceutical business. He arrived at the height of the 1921 famine. When he witnessed the starving bodies and endless fields of parched wheat stubble, he was moved to arrange his first major barter.

On chutzpah alone, Hammer promised the Russians a million bushels of American wheat in exchange for $1 million worth of furs, hides, caviar, and other goods. Actually, he wrote later on, the profit motive was far from his mind. All he could remember was "the cordwood dead waiting to be rolled into their trenchlike graves and the pleading faces of thousands of children at the windows of the special train."

This first barter started Dr. Hammer on a lifetime of advantageous trades, including his fabulous art collection, which began with the ikons and Czarist artifacts he acquired while living in revolutionary Moscow.

What can we learn from these big-time barterers?

1. Barter is a useful device for getting around trading difficulties arising from currency regulations.
2. Barter's flexibility gives it the potential for interfering in normal commercial markets.
3. Barter enables stockholders in mergers to delay paying tax on their sizable profits.
4. Barter can deflate the value of the product so that its cost is estimated, and taxed, at lower than wholesale.
5. Barter is useful as a tax wash.
6. Barter can be the principle means of building tax-free empires through trading up.
7. Barter is a way of dodging the inconvenience of local regulations along international borders, and of seizing the opportunity to play one economy off against another.

Individuals can use barter as advantageously as the big-time barterers. In fact, barter provides you with an effective means of fighting economic oppression caused by corporations and government. However, before you engage in wholesale barter, you have to be aware, as are the corporations and barter barons, of tax laws.

BARTER AND THE IRS

Anyone may so arrange his affairs that his taxes shall be as low as possible; he is not bound to choose that pattern which will best pay the Treasury; there is not even a patriotic duty to increase one's taxes.

—JUDGE LEARNED HAND

The basic IRS position on barter is that it constitutes income as if it were cash. It must be declared and taxes must be paid on it.

Section 61A of the Internal Revenue Code reads as follows:

Except as otherwise provided in this subtitle, gross income means all income from whatever source derived, including (but not limited to) the following items:

It then lists a variety of ways in which people can earn money—everything from fees to alimony—but it does not mention barter. This misleads people. They think that because barter is not specifically mentioned, it is excluded from the concept of taxable income. But they are wrong. *All income from whatever source derived* unequivocably includes barter.

However, the code does have a major section which offers the barterer considerable advantage over the nonbarterer. It is the section that makes it possible for barter barons and horsetraders to build their tax-free pyramids of complex deals without ever having to pay a cent in income tax.

PART III

COMMON NONTAXABLE EXCHANGES, Section 1031: Exchange of Property Held for Productive Use or Investment

a. *Nonrecognition of Gain or Loss from Exchanges Solely in Kind*

No gain or loss shall be recognized if property held for productive use in trade or business or for investment is exchanged solely for property of a like kind to be held either for productive use in trade or business or investment.

This means that any tangible investment, including assets in business, real property, machinery, livestock, equipment for business or investment purposes can be *exchanged in kind without having to pay tax*. Once you sell the investment, however, you must pay capital gains tax.

How do you—a barterer—take advantage of this tax law? Let us suppose you own a piece of rental property that originally cost you $50,000. It is now worth $100,000 and the mortgage has been paid off. If you sold it and pocketed the profit, you would have to pay capital gains tax. But if you find a building on the market for $500,000 that requires a $100,000 down payment, you could offer your property, worth $100,000, as the down payment instead of offering cash. Because both properties are rental units, they are considered like kind. Let us assume your offer is accepted. You have traded up. Your original investment was worth $50,000. You now own a $500,000 building and you have not paid a penny of income tax!

The same principle, of course, applies to pre-Columbian pots, diamonds, pickup trucks, and vegetables. So long as the trade is *in kind*, your profits are safe from the IRS.

There is a second area in the tax code which offers the barterer additional leeway. *Income tax does not have to be paid on gifts which are exchanged.* According to the Supreme Court, "A gift in the statutory sense proceeds from a detached and disinterested generosity out of affection, respect, admiration, charity, or like impulses."

A gift must be devoid of ulterior motive. Now any anthropologist would argue that ulterior motive always is implicit in giving gifts, but fortunately the IRS makes distinctions.

One step removed from the notion of gift is the notion of favor. Business favors are taxable. *But the IRS tends to look the other way when it comes to favors between friends and neighbors. New York* magazine (January 12, 1977) quotes Tom Glynn, assistant to the commissioner of the Internal Revenue Service in Washington, as saying, "If you paint a house for a neighbor and he tends your lawn in return, such favors between friends might not have to be reported. It's impractical for us to tax, and expect people to report, neighbors' doing favors for each other."

Clearly this relaxation certainly benefits the barterer! The terminology of "friends and favors" can be stretched to cover a wide variety of barter experiences, from the direct swap to the complex labor exchange.

However, before attempting to label *all* your exchange activity as gifts or favors, it might be helpful to examine the case of *The Commissioner of Internal Revenue* vs. *Duberstein.* The case began in the 1950s, when Duberstein was audited. It went all the way to the Supreme Court. It is an amusing illustration of the trouble you might run into, should you be too quick to call a barter a gift.

Two men, Berman and Duberstein, transacted a lot of business with each other by phone. They held each other in esteem and respect, and considered each other personal friends. From time to time Duberstein would give Berman names of potential customers. He did this as a favor without expecting compensation. Berman was so appreciative that, "One day, in 1951, Berman called Duberstein and said that the information Duberstein had given him had proved so helpful that he wanted to give the latter a present. Duberstein stated that Berman owed him nothing."

Berman insisted! He wanted to send his dear friend a Cadillac as a thank-you present. Duberstein did not want a Cadillac. He already had a Cadillac! But Berman prevailed, and Duberstein, although he did not ask for it or expect it or even want it, received a Cadillac. He did not include the value of this car in his gross income for 1951, deeming it a gift.

The Supreme Court decided that "despite the characterization of the transfer of the Cadillac by the parties and the absence of any obligation, even of a moral nature, to make it, it was, at bottom, a recompense for Duberstein's past services, or an inducement for him to be of further service in the future."

Therefore, because of the intentions in Berman's mind at the time of giving him the Cadillac, Duberstein was ordered to declare it as income.

Remember, if you have any questions about barter and income tax, consult your tax advisor.

BARTER AND FRAUD

One of the obvious benefits of barter is the ease with which you can ignore recording it. If you do not report it as income, it is very difficult to trace.

Raymond, a dentist in Omaha, Nebraska, is quite open about his modus operandi. "You've got to set up the patient's chart in such a way that an IRS agent cannot tell what it is. You know how most guys get caught? Someone in their office turns them in!" Raymond estimates that one-third of his income goes unrecorded as barter.

There are others, such as the accountant in Nevada who carefully keeps two sets of books. One is for cash records and the other for barter records. The IRS never sees the latter.

What Raymond and the accountant are doing is called fraud.

Fraud though it might be, one of the less publicized but major reasons many people join a barter club is to avoid paying income tax. In order to protect themselves, the clubs tell prospective members that they should not join to avoid paying taxes, but to increase business. They also refer all tax questions to the prospective member's accountant. However, printed pamphlets and orientation discussions include an intricate side-stepping of such direct tax questions as the following:

1. You do not have to pay tax when you belong to a barter club because you are operating as a business, *trading wholesale for wholesale.*
2. You do not pay tax at the time you earn your credit because it has not yet been converted to income; *it is still income owed you.*
3. Once you spend credit, you are obliged to describe it as income. However, many people feel they spend it only on business expenses which are then deductible, so it is really a *tax wash.*
4. You are spending your credit, yes, but you are spending it on *"life's little extras,"* insignificant trivia that does not concern the IRS.
5. At least one barter club has a policy of *shredding computer read-out records,* so no credit-debit files exist after a certain period.

It is not necessary to risk tax fraud in order for barter to improve your economic standing. *The elimination of state sales tax, and the sections regarding nontaxable exchange in kind and nontaxable exchange of gifts,* give the barterer enormous advantage in avoiding the onerous burden of income tax.

Is it possible to avoid income tax altogether through barter? One man seems to have done so.

ONE MAN'S TAX FIGHT

There is one man in the country today who is using barter as a guerrilla tactic in his fight against big government and big business. Karl Hess, a former speech writer for Barry Goldwater, shifted during the latter period of the Vietnam

War from conservatism (and the belief that the least government is the best government) to anarchism (retaining the belief that the least government is the best government).

He is perhaps the most famous, and certainly one of the few who makes the effort to arrange their total economic life around barter. He is a tax resister. As long as the government spends his tax dollars on projects he deems criminal—war, nuclear proliferation, and welfare—he will not pay taxes.

In the *New York Times Magazine*, November 9, 1975, Hess reports that the IRS informed him that it would place a lien against his property and would take 100 percent of the money he earned. In order to avoid paying and to avoid going to jail, Hess simply stopped earning money. He informed the IRS that he would barter. Apparently they told him, "If you get some turnips for your work, we'll take the turnips," but they never have. So royalties for his book *Dear America*, as well as lecture fees and payments for articles, are paid in goods and services.

Bartering has placed Karl Hess back in a "real economy" in which "work is exchanged for work, value is exchanged for value." Learning to do without property has forced him to attend more carefully to other things, "friendship, skills, self-reliance, and active performance rather than obsessive accumulation." When you get into barter, Hess says, "It beats cash all hollow!"

Like Upton Sinclair, Hess recognizes that barter embodies "all our true pioneer virtues—self-reliance, initiative, frugality, equality, neighborliness." And, like Sinclair, Hess recognizes its usefulness in fighting against "megapolism and giantism" in order to build toward a society in which economics is not separated from social philosophy and psychological welfare. Barter is a natural link in an economic overview that is rooted in mutual aid, a respect for limits, a belief in local control, and that is dedicated to the nurturing of humanity within us all.

6.

Is Barter for You?

Harry and Lorraine are a perfectly matched couple. They have weathered their ups and downs with love, good humor, and pragmatism. Now that Harry has retired, they take off for camping trips through Mexico; they indulge in their love of folk art; they put energy into organizations which try to make the world a better place.

They agree on everything . . . except barter.

Harry loves barter. He is an outgoing man who enjoys nothing more than meeting new people, getting good bargains, and tinkering at fix-it jobs where he can do favors in exchange for favors. Through bartering he meets people with whom he ordinarily would never come in contact. The best thing that can happen in our society, says Harry, is anything which encourages contact between individuals.

Lorraine, on the other hand, could not be less interested in bartering. She is shy, reserved, and uncomfortable with strangers. She likes the structure of department stores. She can return things if they are damaged, the prices are clearly marked, and the products are available when she wants them.

She would rather use her energies in other directions, and pay the extra money for the convenience and predictability of monetary transactions.

Clearly, Lorraine is not a born barterer, and there is no reason for her to experience distress; no moral imperative dictating that barter is better or that barterers are better people or that barterers have more fun impel her to change her mind.

But how do you know ahead of time if barter is for you? What if the process reduces you to an anxious wreck, full of guilt about making a good deal, or anger about getting cheated? What if it gets you depressed about the amount of time you have committed to perform your end of the labor exchange, or worried and suspicious that the other people will never do theirs? What if it louses us your bookkeeping? Or brings messy relationships into your life?

It might be helpful to get reassurance from happy barterers. If you don't know any, call someone in the swap column of your local newspaper and ask, "What do you really get out of swapping?" Chances are the person will love to tell you. Another place to find enthusiastic testimonies is *Mother Earth News*, which has a "Successful Swap" section each month filled with letters such as this one:

> We've done a heap of trading . . . most of which has involved livestock. We've swapped two piglets for a milk goat . . . two dry nannies for a white-faced heifer calf. . . . Once we even exchanged a young bull calf for an ole 'clunker' that will probably outlive his youthful counterpart.

But, you say, I live in Bay Elm, New Jersey. What have heifers and goats to do with me? How about this one:

> Our very best swap is now 15 years old and 6′5″ tall. Darach, our son, was "traded" for a dangerous dead elm that was causing lawsuit problems for the new obstetrician in town. (He was poor and could not afford to remove it.) My husband [a tree surgeon] . . . suggested exchanging the work [of removing the tree] for obstetric care for our next child. . . . Nine and a half months later we sealed the deal. . . .

The letters in *Mother Earth News* are refreshing, wholesome, full of folksy charm and good advice. But if you are like most people, you will probably feel that each barter experience is unique. No one else's barter experience will fit your own situation.

What else can you do to decide whether or not you want to get your feet wet—or even your big toe?

You can examine your neighborhood. Certain sections of cities, like certain parts of the country, exude an atmosphere for barter that makes it easy for even the most inhibited beginners.

Do you live in a neighborhood where there are any of the following? (check as many as you know about):

a. food coops
b. community gardens
c. used furniture stores
d. alternative businesses
c. communes (political or spiritual)
e. work collectives
f. free stores
g. concentration of volunteer services
h. geographical hardship
i. college students
j. women's centers
k. free university
l. retired people
m. artists and craftspeople
n. homesteaders
o. child-care centers
p. used car parts
q. swap meets, flea markets, garage sales
r. local swap columns
s. "Western" or "Indian" exhibitions
t. do-it-yourself construction
u. land collectives
v. communication networks
w. barter clubs
x. energy banks
y. baby-sitting coops
z. pot luck dinners

If you can check even one item, there is access to barter at your doorstep. If you can check more than five, you live in an area conducive to barter, and if you decide to try your hand at it, your chances of finding sympathetic, supportive people are high indeed.

But still, you have not figured out whether it is worth your while.

Examine your monthly budget. What is your income? Is

it sufficient to buy everything you want? Certain incomes are blatantly deficient. If you are unemployed, on welfare, living on social security, on scholarship, or anywhere near the official poverty level, you *ought* to try barter. It could bring some very welcome extras into your life.

For the middle class, and those in the 50 percent and above tax brackets, barter is equally worth trying.

If 50 percent of your income is taxed, then your real income basically is half of what you earn before taxes. In order to enjoy your income at its full value, you would have to work twice as hard and earn twice as much, which of course would put you in a higher tax bracket—the familiar vicious circle.

It is even more infuriating when you realize that the $25 per hour you pay the plumber is really $50 of your pretaxed income. Or, if you earn $25 per hour yourself, you have to work two hours in order to pay the plumber for one hour's work!

Have you ever tabulated the amount of extra time you must work and extra money you must earn in order to restore your original wage rate? If you are taxed 20 percent, then your effective wage is 80 percent of what you earn per hour. You must make 125 percent and work one hour and fifteen minutes in order to restore your original earnings.

IN ORDER TO RESTORE ORIGINAL EARNINGS YOU MUST

If your tax rate is (in percent)	then your effective wage is (in percent)	earn (in percent)	work (in hours and minutes)
20	80	125	1:15
25	75	133	1:20
33	67	150	1:30
40	60	167	1:40
50	50	200	2
70	30	333	3:20

(From *Home, Inc.,* by Scott Burns)

Now let us examine what happens if you exchange services with friends.

Your plumbing needs to be fixed. Your friend the plumber

earns $25 per hour. You also earn $25 per hour. You have three choices. You could pay $25, but it makes no sense to work two hours to earn the money to pay the plumber for one hour's work. You could fix it yourself, but you are inept with your hands, and fixing your plumbing would cost you more in time and upset than it would be worth. Or you could barter. Your friend, as a friend, fixes the plumbing and you, as an equivalent favor, help mix mortar and lay bricks for a new patio. You both save more than the nominal cost of paying for someone else's labor; you save the additional amount you would have had to have earned before taxes.

O.K. You acknowledge that regardless of your tax bracket, barter saves you money and/or provides you with otherwise unaffordable goods and services. And if you had a friend who was a plumber, your toilet would be in great shape. But what next? How can you tell whether barter is pertinent to your *immediate* circumstances?

1. Write down all the things on which you spend money, using categories such as the following:

Food	Entertainment
Rent	Hobbies
Utilities	Sports
Transportation	Garden
Education	Reading matter
Personal services	Spiritual/religious
Child care	Household furnishings
Health	Travel
Clothing	Pets
Insurance	Business overhead

(Be specific within each category!)

2. Now make a list of all the things in your life with which you are willing to part.

3. Make a list of all the skills, talents, and special abilities you have.

4. Make another list of the people in your life who either sell goods to you or service you in any way.

5. Can you make any matches between your goods and skills and theirs? Do they need something you have? Can you do something they want? If you are able to mix and match

needs and people on paper, you are already on your way to bartering!

Even though the economic benefits are clear, there are still other factors to take into consideration. It is possible that, like Lorraine, you might be rendered so uncomfortable by the process that no amount of savings would be worth it.

Try participating (not too seriously) in the following personality test in order to determine what your barter profile is. Remember—there is no way to *really* tell unless you try it!

WHAT'S YOUR BARTER QUOTIENT?

1. You are in an expensive, sophisticated department store. The leather wallet you want is scratched, and it is the only one left. You
  a. buy it anyway
  b. decide it's not worth it
  c. find the floor supervisor and ask for a reduction
2. You are in a marketplace in Mexico. The vendor has given you a price for the serape. You know you are supposed to haggle. You
  a. feel uncomfortable, but haggle anyway
  b. feel uncomfortable, even guilty, and pay the full amount
  c. say "too much" and start haggling with gusto
3. Your son-in-law is a terrific auto mechanic. Your car needs a tune-up. You
  a. don't want to impose on him
  b. ask him to do it because you are family
  c. offer him your tickets to next Friday's Knicks game, which he's dying to see, in exchange
4. You see an art deco table lamp in a used furniture store. It's a bargain, but you still can't afford it. You
  a. borrow the money
  b. resent the fact that you can't buy it and are in a bad mood for the rest of the day
  c. offer the shopkeeper your patchwork quilt
5. An old friend comes into your home and admires a moderately priced Oriental basket. You
  a. offer it as a gift immediately
  b. bring the friend the basket instead of wine the next time you are invited for dinner
  c. say thank you and tell your friend where you bought it

6. You are a first-rate electric guitar player. As a result, you are always invited to parties and told to bring your guitar. You

    a. bring it, because they are your friends, but you resent having to be the entertainment factor

    b. figure that if you add up all the eating, drinking, and smoking you do, it balances out

    c. accept the invitations, but refuse to bring the guitar

7. You had a good deal on a load of paint-grade plywood from a friend of a friend who is moving out of town. It turns out only the top piece was paint grade. You can't use it. You

    a. call your friend and raise hell

    b. tell yourself you got what you deserved; next time you'll go to a lumber yard

    c. offer it to your neighbor who is building a darkroom

8. Your family has a K.P. chart. It is your week to clean the bathrooms, a job you hate! Your teen-age son has yard work, which you love. You

    a. trade chores

    b. clean the bathroom because it is your turn

    c. rant and rave that you cannot stand cleaning bathrooms until some sympathetic member of the family offers to do it for you

9. Once a week you eat lunch with fellow office workers. You

    a. compulsively reach for the tab

    b. alternate paying for the tab each week

    c. split the tab each time

10. A funny little man comes up to you and offers you some beans in exchange for your cow. You

    a. avoid the confrontation and walk on without speaking

    b. get angry and scold him for trying to gyp you

    c. figure why not, and make the exchange

Barter Quotient Score

1. a=0;	b=5;	c=10	6. a=5;	b=10;	c=0
2. a=5;	b=0;	c=10	7. a=5;	b=0;	c=10
3. a=0;	b=5;	c=10	8. a=10;	b=5;	c=0
4. a=0;	b=5;	c=10	9. a=0;	b=10;	c=5
5. a=5;	b=10;	c=0	10. a=0;	b=5;	c=10

If you scored:

0 to 20: Stay away from barter. You definitely prefer a predictable, structured system of exchange with carefully delineated boundaries minimizing chances of emotional entanglement. The spontaneity, flexibility, and adventure of barter will be more threatening than gratifying to you.

20 to 40: You prefer traditional routes of exchange. If barter does not happen smoothly, you might find yourself discouraged quickly. But don't let that stop you from following your occasional impulse to make a trade. In small doses, you might not only enjoy it, but find it liberating.

40 to 60: Although you do not go out of your way to barter, you enjoy doing so if the opportunity presents itself. You like the people contact, the sense of doing something out of the ordinary, but you are not willing to take the time to work out trades. By putting such a premium on convenience, you might be losing sight of the forest for the trees. Some of the same energy you spend in coping with the hassles of shopping or in dealing with the repairperson syndrome, could be diverted into working out a barter. Not only would you get what you want, but the time spent getting it would be creative and enjoyable. The more you barter, the easier it becomes and the more convenient it will be.

60 to 80: You are clearly someone who gets a kick out of bartering. Given the odds, you would rather barter than pay cash, and you seek out the opportunity to do so on a hit-or-miss basis. You share many traits with the true barterer (see 80 to 100), but you lack commitment. Perhaps you have not figured out how to integrate barter into your life style. Perhaps you don't think your friends or neighbors would be receptive to long-term exchanges. You are fairly forthright yourself. The problem might be that it has not occurred to you that they are waiting to be asked.

80 to 100: A barterer! You exhibit those traits which barterers consider important in themselves. You have confidence in your own power and the knack for remembering who has or needs what. You are flexible, empathetic, "tuned in" to others' needs, trusting of others, and are willing to play their games if it means getting what you want. You are pragmatic; you have an understanding of value-for-value exchange, a

sense of the theatrical, a relaxed attitude of give and take, a love of adventure.

Painter-sculptor J., a confirmed swapper, describes barter as a "love dance." You understand what he means—the emotional contact, the intuitive moves. You appreciate the rules of the contest, if it is a contest, and the esthetics of the perfect trade.

J. learned to barter as a teen-ager on a ranch. The moves of this love dance come as naturally to him as waltzing does to the Viennese. But what about the awkward adult, trying it for the first time, tripping over feet, becoming a fool on the dance floor?

If you are not quite certain that you're ready to go out and barter in public, the best thing to do is practice at home until you build your confidence. The next time your son or daughter wants to borrow the car for a Saturday night date, tell him or her you are open to barter—a car wash in exchange. When Aunt Sally admires your crocheted shawl, instead of offering outright to make her one, tell her you're open to barter—her homemade preserves in exchange.

There are two key phrases to repeat: *"Have you ever thought of trading?"* and *"I'm open to barter."*

If no situations arise spontaneously, create some yourself. Play-act with family and friends. For example:

You sell radios. How would you approach your grocer with the idea of trade?

You drive a truck. You want some jewelry. What are you going to do?

A long-time friend calls. She has left her husband and would like to stay at your house for a while. You are trying to finish your computer programming course, you have three children and you are none too neat. How do you work out a deal with your friend?

Here is an unusual experiment one woman conducted—her own "play" use of barter to liberate herself from the confines of a meager monthly paycheck and an unfulfilling job.

Sandy Davis, a proud and talented artist, was struggling for financial independence as a supermarket cashier in an upper-middle-class neighborhood in Sherman Oaks, California. She resented the rude, contemptuous manner in which the tennis-togged shoppers treated her. One day she fantasized that cherry tomatoes would become the only medium of exchange, and she would corner the market.

Because she was in a performance workship, she was able to develop this fantasy for a production. She studied market-manipulation techniques and on the day of the performance she acquired all the cherry tomatoes she could buy, beg or steal and placed them in an enormous basket. She came on-stage in her cashier's uniform with her basket of tomatoes and successfully manipulated the audience into desiring these tomatoes. Pretty soon, the audience was willing to spend any amount of money to get them. Sandy raised and lowered the value as she saw fit. However, she was not satisfied with this mini–economic system. She felt alienated from the audience. She wanted to know who they were, and what they had to offer for the tomatoes besides money. So she began to barter.

People responded enthusiastically. They stopped hoarding tomatoes in case the "market" went up. They offered skills for as many or as few cherry tomatoes as made sense to them. Sandy bartered not on the basis of profit, but on the basis of personal value.

After that evening, Sandy felt wonderful! Previously, she could only imagine acquiring money by working in rigid, salaried situations. In front of the audience, performing, she saw other possibilities.

She started bartering in real life. Though she continued to work at the supermarket, she began bartering her art work for the luxuries she wanted but could not afford. The economic system was no longer an oppressive factor in her life. It had become something to play with, something she could manipulate more easily because of barter.

Sandy's unique barter performance is not meant to be taken as a literal suggestion for would-be barterers to duplicate. What she actually did was create a metaphor about barter and its effect on the individual.

Through this metaphor she had an experience common to barterers who discover that they enjoy bartering, other people are receptive to it, and barter makes a pleasant difference in their lives.

Once you barter, you will see opportunities everywhere. Without trepidation you will approach optometrists, dressmakers, architects, and roadside innkeepers, asking, "Are you open to barter?" Evelyn Harris, "The Barter Lady," who wrote a book telling how she survived the Depression through barter, said that with the application of persistent ingenuity, she even was able to pay local taxes in barter!

You might find yourself so committed to the concept of equal exchange of goods and services that you try to persuade others to join you. If so, it will be the first step on your way to making the economic status quo more responsive and serviceable through barter.

7.

Some Things to Watch Out For

Unlike the Trobriand Islanders, Americans are not conditioned from birth to seek parity in exchange. Because we are products of a heritage that stresses material success, profit making, and competition, the chances of bartering with someone who will try to take advantage of you are reasonably high. This is not to say that everyone will be out to take advantage of you. Barterers are for the most part honest, friendly people who are looking for good deals and nothing more.

It is wise to acquaint yourself with those areas in which scams, con jobs, and mistreatment most often occur, and to learn what to avoid before you've made a serious barter mistake.

Less dramatic but equally as frustrating as the scam are the organizational inequities found in some of the barter clubs. These too require examination. With proper knowledge, you can circumvent many trouble spots that cause dissatisfaction among club members.

Used cars, real estate, and stolen goods are the most problematic trades you are likely to encounter in individual barter. Real estate scams, misuse of barter scrip, and inability to spend credit are the key sources of problems in the barter clubs.

Behind both individual and group barter exploitation lies the psychology of someone who figures a fool is a fool, and that if you get taken, it is your own fault. Fortunately, this psychology is not the norm. But it's an exception that can sour your bartering experience if you do not take pains to learn what to watch out for.

INDIVIDUAL BARTER PITFALLS

1. **Used Cars.** Though there are not as many horsetraders as there once were, the horsetrading tradition is carried on by the used-car dealer. Chicanery in vehicle trading can be carried rather far because almost everyone needs or wants a car and most people understand little about how cars operate.

It's hard to believe that people trade perfectly good cars for broken-down ones, but it happens all the time. One trader from Houston, Texas, describes how in his "less savory past" he used to sit in front of his "auto handling service" and make corrupt deals all day long. With a highly developed patter of swift talk, he could convince people to exchange their 1958 356 B Porsche in mint condition for a broken-down '41 Cadillac and a '61 Fiat that didn't run.

Another car dealer, whom we will call Ivan, takes even greater advantage of people's ignorance. He plays a game with hungry newcomers to San Diego who need to sell their cars quickly because they have not yet found a job.

Ivan's car deals involve cash, but he works the same routine with trade. The game is instructional because its basic principles are followed by dishonest traders in every field—scuba gear, camera equipment, appliances, and others.

Ivan calls his friend Alfonso one day and said, "I've got a kid from Iowa with a 1929 Alfa Romeo coupé. He says it's a classic. He wants sixteen hundred dollars. Should I take it?"

Alfonso knows the game. "Bring it to my shop," he says.

Ivan explains to the Iowan that his friend is a reputable mechanic. They drive the car over. "Worthless," announces Alfonso.

The Iowan is mortified. His price drops to $400, but Ivan insists on $300. He says no; he is sure he can get at least $400 for the Alfa elsewhere. He will put ads in the paper.

That afternoon, Ivan calls up all the papers and puts his own ad in, saying he has a 1929 Alfa Romeo coupé selling at $125. He gives a phony address. The next day, having received no calls, and broken-hearted, the Iowan returns, ready to make the deal.

Ivan counts on the fact that his victims won't bother to verify the worth of their own car by asking reputable dealers for an estimate. (A car is usually worth twice the amount that a bona fide car dealer offers.) In addition, he assumes they will never question the legitimacy of his pal "the mechanic," who presumes to be an expert but is actually cooperating with Ivan.

The same situation exists with boats. People get quite excited about the idea of trading for a boat, but often know nothing about them. While a boat can look beautiful on the outside, the wood can be rotting underneath the paint. There is no way of knowing if the boat is watertight unless you actually take it into the water, preferably in company with a knowledgeable boat surveyor who will make a thorough examination before you take it in trade.

2. Stolen goods. There is an excellent chance that you will be offered something "hot" or at least "warm" during your bartering career. It will be an item that is presented as a terrific bargain by a quiet trader who volunteers no extra information, and if you are not a suspicious person it might never occur to you that it has been stolen.

Aside from any moral reservations you might have about receiving stolen goods, it is possible that you, unwittingly, could run into difficulty should you ever try to sell or barter them. Police agents frequent flea markets, swap meets, and second-hand stores, inspecting serial numbers on typewriters, cameras, and the like. Your terrific bargain could wind up confiscated as stolen goods.

3. Real estate fraud. During the 1920s, land booms were a feverish source of speculation and misrepresentation. Swamps were sold as suburbs, desert land was sold as a tropical resort, and bogus promises of paradise in Florida and California caused thousands of Midwesterners to lose their life's savings. Land fraud is not as spectacular a problem today, but for the many innocent victims who buy vacation lots where none exists, it is just as destructive.

Victims of real estate fraud are often people considering a vacation or retirement house in an unfamiliar resort location, such as the mountains or the desert. These victims usually already have their own homes, where they have been living for a number of years, dutifully paying off the mortgage. Unfamiliar with the ins and outs of real estate value, they use these homes in trade. The young and those with no homes of their own will have their vans or motor homes taken by real estate hucksters as down payment.

In either case, prospective clients are taken to see "their" land if they wish, but without accurate surveyor's maps, they never see its specific location. When they finally have the title deed, they discover that their lot is competely inaccessible. Moreover, when the charming "developer" and/or agent was there to explain all the amenities, they lost sight of the fact that none really existed. This fact hits home *after* they've bought or traded for the property. They have fooled themselves into thinking they were making a tremendous investment for the future. In reality, they gave up their home and wound up with nothing.

Antelope Valley, the high desert outside of Los Angeles, recently has been a notorious location for land fraud. Citing as a certainty the tenuous possibility that an airport serving the LA area was going to be built, developers played up Antelope Valley as the next San Fernando Valley. Preying upon people's natural desire to make a shrewd investment, clever hucksters sold or traded nonexistent or undeveloped lots.

4. Miscellaneous. Barter cons flourish with every new fad. A couple of years ago, during the height of the popularity of Indian jewelry, non-Indian "Indian traders" passed off new, factory-made silver and turquoise jewelry as "pawnshop heirlooms." At every Western trade show, people swapped valuable goods to receive in exchange fake Indian squash-blossom necklaces, rings, and belt buckles. (If you plan on trading in the Southwest, you should know that barter is an integral part of Navaho culture. There is no way a tourist can barter for an Indian object and come out ahead when trading with a Navaho.)

The same caution applies to any fad—pukka-shell necklaces, African masks, organic fertilizers, etc.

GROUP BARTER PITFALLS

The pitfalls of individual barter might cause you to seek refuge in an organized trade club, where you assume you are trading with peers, well-meaning and honest people like yourself, looking to save a little money and to beat inflation. Unfortunately, you are just as vulnerable in a barter club as you are out of one. As one disgruntled member pointed out, "There's lots of people with larceny in their souls, and there's nothing to stop them from joining the clubs!"

The worst clubs invariably are the ones that have not solved their structural problems. They either have insufficient backing, do not regulate the amount of members who go on standby, permit rampant price inflation and scrip manipulation, or they do not limit the number of 50 percent cash members.

Hand in hand with these structural problems often is the much more pernicious institutionalization of scams—real estate scams, insurance scams, misuse of barter scrip.

This is not to say that all trade clubs engage in underhanded activity or are beset with structural difficulty. There are clubs, such as Los Angeles's Business Exchange, Hilton Exchange, and others, that consistently retain their reputation for honesty and for satisfying the needs of their membership.

1. Club failure. Many barter clubs are started, but not all flourish. Hilton of Hilton Exchange observes that twenty or thirty trade clubs have been in and out of business in Southern California during the last twenty years.

What does this mean for the barterer in a trade club?

A club needs sufficient financial backing through its beginning phases to insure its eventual success. This is true of any business. But unlike a regular business, the club member suffers risks as well as the investor.

All too often, after clubs are started and members are recruited and given scrip in exchange for their goods, the club suddenly folds. Members are stuck with handfuls of worthless scrip. The members have assumed risks that will never garner them profit should the club succeed, but will cause them loss should it fail.

2. Dry-up/Standby Phenomenon. When you join a club, word spreads quickly to the "in group," leaving those members who rely on the newsletter or directory far behind. You find yourself deluged with trade requests. Pleased by the attention, you tend to trade out your goods or services indiscriminately. Finally, you realize that you have amassed more than enough credit. The time has come to spend it.

Unfortunately, everyone you call is "dried up." They, too, have an abundance of credit and have taken advantage of a clause which all clubs have—the standby clause. Once you have over a certain amount of credit, you go on standby and stop trading until you have spent the excess credit. The standby clause is a precaution to prevent imbalances on the side of credit. However, it is very frustrating when you pore over the directory and can find no one willing to trade with you.

The trade director tells you to be patient. After six months of persistent patience, the director offers you a compensatory deal—real estate, insurance, due bills to a hotel in Las Vegas. But what you really wanted were auto mechanics to fix your car and a carpenter to remodel the maid's room into a guest bedroom. You have the uncomfortable feeling that the director is trying to palm off items that benefit the club more than they benefit you.

3. Price inflation and scrip manipulation. Some people think belonging to barter clubs gives them license to charge twice in scrip what they would in cash for the same goods and services. This makes it impossible for the honest members who do not double their prices to come out even.

Because of price inflation, the value of the scrip becomes unstable. If members are charging twice what they ordinarily would if they were using cash, the value of the scrip decreases by half. If a lot of inflating goes on at one club, and very little at another, the scrip of club A will be worth less than the scrip of club B. There are a certain number of people who buy and sell scrip much the same way money traders buy and sell currency.

One scrip manipulator reports that he belonged to club A, which had stable scrip that was desirable. He traded it for the scrip of club B on an eight-to-ten ratio. Club B scrip, he commented, "bounced around like a rubber ball." He intended to hang onto it until its value went up and then sell it for cash, or for another club's scrip.

Needless to say, this kind of manipulation only hurts

the straightforward member who has joined the barter club, in part, to get away from the ups and downs of dollar currency.

4. 50 percent cash membership. Fifty percent cash memberships are held by people who are in businesses that require a certain amount of cash expenditure to cover the cost of goods. They are usually retailers who cannot or will not commit to a 100 percent barter program.

This means that when you go into their store, you pay 50 percent in cash and 50 percent in trade, so a $20 shirt will cost you $10 in money and $10 in trade credit. All too often, the retailer jacks up the cost of the shirt for the trade customers, or adds a "service fee" for the inconvenience of dealing with club vouchers. At this point, the shirt costs you more than if you purchased it in a store, because in addition to the regular retail price you are paying extra in trade credit.

5. Theft. Structural and organizational problems can be ironed out. It is more difficult to regulate the unethical practices that permeate some trade clubs. Because trade clubs are cresting a popularity wave, they are attracting a small number of sophisticated racketeers and a somewhat larger number of unsophisticated but greedy opportunists. These people view the trade club as nothing more than a vehicle for systematizing scams.

Club owners have prior access to the names and merchandise of new members. There is nothing to prevent dishonest owners from considering the club their own private warehouse. One trade director finally quit when she realized that her boss and his wife would pick up merchandise, such as stereophonic equipment, jewelry, and furs from new members, give them trade credit and then sell the merchandise and pocket the money. Nobody knew. The member with the merchandise had received credit, and when other members called up to trade, they were told the goods had dried up. Nobody suspected the owners of stealing from their own club.

Another form of theft occurs when club owners print scrip without having actual backing in trade credit. This is tantamount to counterfeiting. A former manager of a northwestern club comments that the major problem with that club was its owner, who printed up scrip whenever he needed it and used it to get whatever he wanted. He never put anything back into the club and eventually drained its resources dry.

Very often, separate businesses are owned by the same people who own the barter clubs. These businesses are supported entirely by the misuse of barter club assets. For example, the owner of one less than ethical club in the West had another business that required a lot of printing. He signed a printer as a member in his club, and used that printer to do all the printing for his other business. He paid the printer in scrip, with no cost to him or his business. The profits from the business went into his private bank account. And as owner of the barter club, he was never called in to account for overspending.

6. Real estate. One of the biggest complaints about barter clubs stems from the pressure to buy valueless real estate.

One woman told a reporter for the *Los Angeles Times* that after she and her husband, a carpenter, accrued $500 in credit, they could not spend it. "We told them we were having trouble spending the money, and now they're trying to get us to buy a piece of property, to use our credit as down payment. But it's a real poor piece of property—there's no easement or access to it."

An optometrist who had trouble spending his $14,000 worth of credit (accumulated within the first three months of joining!) told the same reporter, "I was offered all kinds of real estate deals that didn't smell right."

The bigger barter clubs all have their own real estate divisions. They deal in the trading of homes, rental property, commercial property—everything from small stores to big hotels. Most of the activity involves big-time traders and most of it is legitimate.

However, some of it is not. One barter club had purchased acres of barren wasteland in Texas. The land was subdivided in the early 1960s and its anticipated development never occurred. Dirt roads are overgrown with tumbleweed. The two water wells are dry and missing their mechanical pumps. The official brochure indicates that the lots are worth $1,000 each, according to current Texas real estate value. But it goes on to suggest that a more reasonable price, given the delay in the subdivision, is $850 per lot. The barter club paid only $35 per lot, and now is touting them to its members as a terrific bargain at $850, acquirable through trade credit. Because the club in question has its own advertising division, it can puff up this special deal and convince members who have no place to spend their trade credit that this is a sound real estate investment.

With more expensive property, a member's down payment might be made in trade credit, but the monthly payments are made in cash. Often the members don't realize this ahead of time. Meanwhile, because all the wheeling and dealing is in the form of trades, clubs pay no capital gains tax on any of their highly profitable real estate transactions.

Club management can combine its knowledge of members' finances with its easy access to partner-linked companies and use this combination to take further advantage.

According to a private investigator who was researching the activities of a club in California, the club's director, scouting around for property to acquire, discovered that a couple in the club was selling their house, which had a $30,000 mortgage against $60,000 equity, with no second loans. The club director wanted the house, agreed to assume the $30,000 mortgage and upped the down payment, promising it in trade. He then went to a partner who is also on the board of an insurance company. The partner talked to one of his insurance policyholders who, he knew from the record, had a little extra cash to invest. He convinced the policyholder to take seconds on this piece of property.

While the house was in the club's escrow division, the two partners pocketed the $30,000 in cash loans (paying no taxes because loans are not taxable), and then defaulted on the mortgage. The policyholder who took the seconds was left holding the property. The members who sold the house, since they were not given cash right away, were left with nothing!

7. Insurance rebates. Barter clubs are frequently linked with insurance companies through overlapping partnerships. This makes the club member an easy target for insurance salespeople. No great damage is done if you purchase insurance, but you are, in fact, being exploited in the following manner:

a. You have accumulated $3,000 in credit that you can't

spend. It is easier, therefore, for a salesman to persuade you to buy an insurance policy, even though you do not need one.

b. You pay $3,000 in credit as the first year's premium payment on a $50,000 policy. After the first year, however, the company will not accept credit payments. Your subsequent payments will be in cash.

c. The club converts your $3,000 in credit to $3,000 in cash and sends it to the insurance company.

d. Within thirty days, the club, not you, receives a 125 percent cash rebate! (Rebates are illegal, but common.)

e. In essence, the club has sold your trade credit for cash at a profit, which it then puts in the private bank accounts of the few who are involved.

8. Paychecks. How your barter club pays its employees might not seem important, but if unhappy employees start taking the management to the labor board or to unemployment insurance officials for the redressing of wrongs, you might find that there is an injunction on your barter club. This prevents you from further trade.

Employees are usually paid in trade, with a small amount of cash slipped under the table. If they lose their job, they are unable to collect unemployment, or even to sue for unpaid back wages.

The foundation of a barter club where employees are paid with indiscriminately manufactured scrip is shaky, to say the least. Like a house of cards, one strong breath from agencies regulating labor and unemployment could blow the whole enterprise away—leaving you, once again, with computer read-outs full of accumulated credit worth no more than a bundle of Monopoly money.

9. Franchises. The possibility for misuse of funds exists within the franchise framework because the parent club handles all the bookkeeping in its computer. Credits and debits are tabulated at the parent club and then distributed to the franchises. Absence of local control makes communication about errors in statements difficult. If the parent club is so inclined, it can create a series of small errors in its favor which will remain undetected for months.

A second misuse of the franchise system occurs when a

franchise is set up merely to be exploited by the parent club. This happened not so long ago when one California club sent a salesperson south to open up another area of the state. He did a good job. Three hundred legitimate businesses joined. Members of the parent club then traveled to the newly opened area by the carload, and spent thousands of credit trade crecks. But when the new members came north to spend all that trade credit, they discovered they couldn't. Every place they went to was on standby. The parent club had dried up long ago. They all suffered heavy losses, and two men, dealers in appliances and stereos, went bankrupt.

Reportedly, these men are now trying to file a class-action suit against the club that bankrupted them. It will be a costly and time-consuming process. It is hoped that the suit will be successful, and thus prevent similar exploitation in the future.

There are steps you can take to prevent yourself from getting hurt in barter situations.

There are two general rules in barter:

1. Know what you want
2. Know what to look for

These rules apply to everything from a chain saw to a trade club. But they are easier said than done. Let us examine how to follow these rules, first in the context of individual barter and second in the context of a barter club.

INDIVIDUAL BARTER PRECAUTIONS

1. Consult an expert. Whether you are swapping for a car, an Oriental rug, a painting, or a camera, it behooves you to find an expert who can tell you whether the object at hand is all that its owner claims it to be. However much experience you have had in bartering, no one is an expert in every field. It might be a little extra trouble, and it might strain the negotiations slightly, but in the long run, consultation will save you a great deal of misery.

Take a car to a reputable mechanic. Take an antique to a licensed antique dealer. Take a painting to a gallery or a museum. Take electrical appliances to a repair shop. If the owner objects, you have cause for suspicion and you should drop the barter.

If you cannot locate an expert, consult books and catalogues to determine fair value. Using the Sears Roebuck catalogue, the Blue Book for car prices, the "Shooters Bible" (if you trade guns) and the library, you will be able to research your swaps thoroughly enough so that no one will be able to take advantage of you.

2. **Check your instincts.** Are you comfortable with the way the swap is proceding? If you have the least doubt, slow down and try to figure out why.

Ask a few questions.

Ask the other person why he or she decided to swap this object. Carefully observe the response. An honest person often has trouble lying. If the response is awkwardness or hesitation, or a series of improbable explanations, you may suspect that something is wrong.

Ask where the object was originally obtained. If the answer is vague, it could mean that the object is "hot." This would be particularly plausible if you were bartering for a fur, radio, clock, tape recorder, TV, or some other commonly stolen item.

Observe how the other person feels about the barter. Overanxious? In a hurry?

Your instincts are your most important guide to whether or not you are getting a good deal. Learn to trust them.

3. **Know what you are getting in real estate.** This rule applies to barter clubs as well as individual barter deals. Anytime someone offers to give you a "charming desert home" in exchange for your perfectly good, albeit old, city bungalow, check out the property. Make sure the surveyors have surveyed it; examine the geology report; determine the zoning; locate the access roads, water lines, sewage and power lines; talk to your lawyer. Don't be fooled! A lot of people are and their cases fill the offices of city, county, and state agencies that handle hundreds of real estate scams a year. *Never trade anything for a piece of real estate unless you know exactly what you are getting.*

GROUP BARTER PRECAUTIONS

If the evils of the cash economy are merely duplicated by barter clubs, there is no reason for belonging to one. A well-run club needs owners and trade directors with integrity and intelligence, who will keep a balance between the credits and debits of the membership, prevent price inflation and scrip manipulation, and insure a reasonable quantity of goods and services so members are able to trade when they want to.

How do you know if the club you are about to join fits this description?. Find out! Select your barter club very carefully or it will prove to be a disappointing experience.

1. Check with active members before you join the club. Find out the following:

> **a.** Is the accounting system adequate? Does it keep accurate records of credit and debit? Does it arrive promptly?
>
> **b.** Are earned credits spendable or are the majority of credits on standby?
>
> **c.** Is the membership generally content or dissatisfied? Why?

2. Make certain the club publishes a directory. This is important. With it, you will be able to contact members *while* you are investigating the club. Also, according to Mr. McConnel of Business Exchange, the absence of a directory could indicate that the club is a blind with no other purpose than to collect the initial cash joining fees.

Moreover, once you have joined the club, you will want to increase your sales. A directory will insure that all the members know you have joined, and not just selected members who have asked the director for something you specifically can supply. Clubs that do not publish directories claim to protect their members—but from whom?

3. Double-check the reputation of the club by calling the Better Business Bureau and the state commission on corporations. The Better Business Bureau will have records containing any complaints that might have been filed. The state commission on corporations will have records that contain notifications of injunctions against the club, plus other evidence of faulty business practices.

4. Talk to club management. Once you have your member response and public record information, sit down and interview the club's management. Brush aside their sales pitch. They may attempt to answer your questions before you can ask them so that the stickier areas of club policy go unnoticed. If there is any aspect of the club that is unclear to you, keep on pursuing until you clarify it.

5. **Check your instincts.** Do you feel you are being hustled? Why? Does the trade director make you feel uncomfortable? Be direct. Say so. It is better to express all your reservations *before* you have paid the nonreturnable joining fee than after.

Barter clubs are businesses. Their primary function is to earn money for the people running them. This means they are not democratic organizations. You do not have an equal voice in determining policy, nor do you share in the profits of the club as a whole. You pay your dues and your commissions, and you take what you can get in trade. Though the club offers you considerable financial benefits, your membership in the club offers it even more—otherwise you wouldn't be there. (One club values "each warm body at $850, even if it's on standby!")

Having made certain that no aspect of the organization remains a mystery, you can decide with some degree of wisdom whether this is the barter club for you.

If you are interested in joining a barter club, have checked with members in the directory, called the Better Business Bureau and the state commission on corporations, and talked to management, and you still are not satisfied, your other recourse is to start your own club.

8.

Start Your Own: A How-to Guide for Setting Up a Barter Group

The best way to start bartering is to just go out and do it. After a while, you see barter possibilities everywhere. Without trepidation you approach optometrists, dressmakers, grocers, and roadside innkeepers. But how about your friends or neighbors? Within a relatively small radius of where you live exists the possibility of having a genuine bartering group.

The Stanford Research Institute's study on voluntary simplicity stated that 4 to 5 million adults fully and wholeheartedly live a life of voluntary simplicity. A poll taken by Louis Harris in 1975 reported that 78 percent of the American people would opt for a change of life style rather than endure the risks of continuing inflation and unemployment. Voluntary simplicity and change of life style certainly could include bartering. It only takes one person to get a barter group going. That person could be you.

However, before you plunge in, sit down and think about what it is you want to do.

Do you want a baby-sitting exchange? Are you interested in a chicken-pig-goat livestock swapping market? Do you fancy a once-a-month artisans' craft exchange? Are you inclined toward rotation of laundry, van washing, house cleaning and bill paying?

There are neighborhood coops and statewide networks. There are big barter agencies and little barter groups. Prototypes for all different kinds exist. They can point out different directions for you, but only you can decide where you want to go.

Ask yourself the following basic questions:

1. For whom are you organizing the barter group?
2. What will be the nature and scope of goods and services involved?
3. What geographic area are you including?
4. How formal or informal will the club be?
5. What are its specific organizational principles?
6. How will you determine parity?
7. To what extent are you interested in linking or networking with complementary organizations?

Some of these questions will be answered automatically once you decide whether you are having a neighborhood exchange or a large-scale operation servicing diverse interest groups. Other questions will require research: discussion with potential exchange members, exploration of advantages and disadvantages of public and private funding, definition of obligations, consultation with accountants and lawyers.

Let us suppose, for simplicity's sake, that you decide to establish either one of two kinds of exchanges—a small, informal neighborhood exchange or a formally structured, nonprofit, incorporated exchange.

NEIGHBORHOOD EXCHANGE

There is nothing easier than creating a small-scale bartering network for yourself. All you need are a few friends and neighbors, some exchangeable skills, and a certain degree of goodwill. With a minimum of effort, you can achieve major economic and emotional gains.

If you contact five people, find out what skills they have, what they need, and what chores they would like to share, you will discover that merely by making this information available, you have set up a framework for barter.

For example, if the five people are members of families on your block, all with children and all with heavy weekly shopping to do, a simple trade could be arranged in terms of child care and shopping. One person would be responsible for the week's shopping for everyone. Another would assume child-care duties during that period. The others would be free until their turn came up.

The creation of a more ambitious neighborhood or friendship exchange will probably follow on the heels of the success of this initial endeavor. How do you do it?

First, you have to know your neighbors.

Familiarize yourself with the nature of their skills and assess their attitudes toward the notion of sharing, their willingness to assume responsibility, and their honesty in carrying out their part of any transaction.

If you need help determining these things, here are some questions you can ask. The following informal survey will help you know whether or not your neighbors are genuinely interested:

1. Because of the tight money situation, a lot of people have started to barter goods and services with each other, often in the form of barter groups or labor exchanges. This means they trade or swap goods or labor with each other, instead of paying each other cash. Have you heard of any of this going on?

2. How long have you lived on this block?

3. Judging by your own experience, how well do you think the neighbors know each other? Why is that?

4. Have you ever done any trading or swapping? If yes, what kind?

5. Do you rely on friends to help out with household repairs, gardening, big parties, child care, transportation, legal or medical advice? Do they rely on you?

6. When you have things you no longer need, you
    a. give it away   c. trade it
    b. sell it   d. throw it away

7. Has the tight money situation affected your attitude toward paying for goods and services? If so, do you
    a. complain more   c. repair instead of replace
    b. cut back   d. recycle old things

8. Have you heard of food coops? Rate them on a scale of 1 to 10 in terms of
    a. savings   c. convenience
    b. quality   d. social experience

9. If you cannot afford something, would you rather
    a. buy it on credit   c. borrow it
    b. go without   d. trade for it

10. Has the energy shortage caused you to change the ways in which you use energy? How so?

11. What percentage of your relationships with neighbors would you describe as:

a. friendly   **c.** nodding
b. casual   **d.** strangers

12. Has there ever been a neighborhood crisis that brought you together? What was the result of that experience?

13. Do you ask anyone on the block to watch your house while you are away? Do they ask you?

14. Have you ever lent equipment to anyone on the block? On a scale of 1 to 10, how would you rate this experience?

15. Have you ever borrowed equipment from anyone on the block? On a scale of 1 to 10, how would you rate this experience?

16. What kind of office, gardening, shop, or household equipment do you own?

17. How would you respond to the idea of making these tools available to your neighbors, who would be making theirs available to you? Rate your response on a scale of 1 to 10 by category:

a. office   **c.** shop
b. gardening   **d.** household
                       e. recreational

18. What are your major reasons for this reaction?

19. FOR YOUR REFERENCE ONLY

a. lack of trust	**a.** trust
b. lack of time	**b.** spare time
c. unfair distribution of tools	**c.** fair distribution
d. unequal notions of responsibility	**d.** equal responsibility
e. different values because of politics, ethics, life style	**e.** shared values
f. lack of economic need	**f.** economic need
g. inconvenience	**g.** convenience
h. tools require special skills	**h.** willing to teach skills
i. not a joiner	**i.** sense of community

20. What would make you feel more comfortable about the idea?

21. Do you feel you are more open or closed to the idea of tool and equipment sharing than other members of your household? What about labor exchange?

22. Do you think your neighbors would have similar responses?

23. If a neighborhood barter group were started, do you think it would improve relationships or increase friction?
24. If a neighbor approached you with the idea of starting a tools and service exchange, how would you respond?
25. Would you help organize it?

Second, invite your neighbors and other interested parties to an introductory meeting.

At this meeting, your objective will be to explain why belonging to a barter group is to everyone's advantage. Your strongest argument, of course, is the financial savings enjoyed by all members of such a group. Nobody will dispute this. But there might be someone who feels time is more valuable. If so, explain that you often have to work twice the amount of time in order to be earning the income after taxes that you would be earning before taxes (see page 73).

Next, point out the support system engendered by an exchange. Whether or not you speak about this in terms of "extended family" is less important than emphasizing that we all seek interconnection, that most of us want reliable people around in case we need them, and that if we examine our common experience, we probably will not find as much support in our everyday lives as we would like.

Third, your group must tackle the more complex organizational problems.

Normally the small-scale neighborhood barter group serves three important functions: it provides information about available skills and equipment; it establishes rules which govern the exchange of skills and equipment; it settles any disputes which might arise.

These functions apply whether the group adopts the structure of a mini–energy bank or whether it serves as a clearinghouse for direct exchange.

As a clearinghouse, it provides information necessary for barter transactions, but does not keep track of the bartering. This is the responsibility of the individuals involved.

A *mini–energy bank* makes possible indirect exchange. It accepts deposits and withdrawals of "energy" or "labor" or "skills" in much the same way a bank accepts deposits and withdrawals of money. Members build up credit by doing labor and they deplete credit or accrue debit by receiving other members' labor.

If the group is organized along the lines of a mini–energy bank, it must allocate responsibility for the credit-debit record keeping. The job could be assigned on a rotating basis, shared equally by all, or could remain in the hands of a competent bookkeeper who would be reimbursed for this work with labor credit.

If the group functions as an information clearinghouse, it must decide how to distribute the information. Is there a file box in a convenient location to which everyone can refer? Do you send out a newsletter listing skills needed and skills available? Do you set up a phone system with a rotating person on duty who matches requests?

The group should keep its operating tasks to a minimum. Except where expertise or consistency is crucial, these tasks should be shared by all.

Every barter group will incur expenses. The group can pay for them through dues or on an ad hoc community basis, but it is necessary to discuss and agree on both the nature of the expenses and the methods of paying them.

ESTABLISHING PARITY

A primary problem your group will face is one of establishing parity. If some members feel an hour of their labor is more valuable than an hour of labor performed by others, the group as a whole will have to arrive at an equitable joint assessment.

There are at least three standard solutions.

1. All labor is equal
2. Market value equivalents
3. Skilled-unskilled ratio

The first requires the belief by all that everyone's need is equal and so is everyone's labor. One hour of my time is worth one hour of your time, no matter what the disparity between our educational backgrounds, training, and experience. What we all do is equally valuable for the other. Parity is self-evident and uncomplicated.

At the other extreme is the use of commercial market rates translated into work-hour credits. Though this solution might be comfortable to some, and offers much of the same financial benefits, it does nothing to transform economic relationships between people.

A third solution is to divide parity along skilled and unskilled lines at a fixed ratio; for example, one hour of skilled labor (plumbing, legal, dental) equals two hours of unskilled labor (yard work, baby-sitting, transportation). The definition of skilled versus unskilled might vary with individuals. Why is a good baby-sitter less skilled than a good auto mechanic? Presumably the group can determine for itself what it values as developed skills and what it is willing to call unskilled. Then it can work out the ratio between the two.

EQUIPMENT

The question of equipment might be an issue in the exchange of certain skills. If parity has been determined on an equal hour-for-hour basis, or on a fixed-ratio basis, the cost of equipment and its depreciation must be figured into the equation. That way you will avoid complaints from a member with a bulldozer who gets no more credit for an hour's work than a member using someone else's hose and rake.

Along these lines, members who incur monetary expense as part of their job should be reimbursed by the person for whom the job is done. A photographer is reimbursed for the cost of paper and chemicals, an electrician for the cost of copper wire. Otherwise, the barter relationship bogs down in complex attempts to balance out the cash aspects of everyone's exchanges.

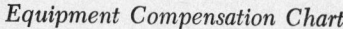

Equipment Compensation Chart

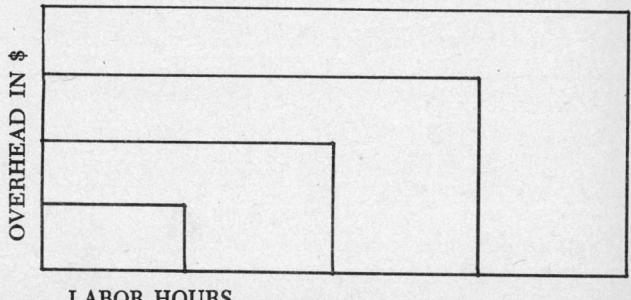

SMALL-SCALE BARTER GROUP

One example of a successful small-scale barter group is the Ocean Exchange, started by Susie and Ken Morrison of Manhattan Beach, California. Ken is a thirty-five-year-old history professor who was recently denied tenure because of budget cutbacks, and who is trying to finish his book on the Armenians' role in the history of California agricultural towns. Susie, a former modern dancer, has gone back to school to study architecture. They have two small children, and live in a cottage designed by Susie that is located in a relaxed beachfront neighborhood. Community feeling in Manhattan Beach runs high, and people meet regularly for Sunday volleyball games.

Ken and Susie, motivated by a tight budget and an even tighter schedule, wanted to transform the neighborhood's casual give-and-take atmosphere into something more structured, something upon which they could depend.

Not only were they interested in skilled and unskilled task sharing, but they wanted to exchange tools and recreational equipment as well. Their motives were fairly selfish. They could not afford a set of skill saws needed to remodel the baby's room. On the other hand, they had a perfectly good power lawn mower which they never used, and were willing to share.

At the meeting they organized, enthusiasm ran high, until one woman admitted that she would feel awkward about letting others use her expensive cameras. The group then decided to lay down the following rules for the use of equipment:

1. Tools used frequently by their owners would not be part of the pool.
2. Equipment which requires special handing would not be part of the pool.
3. Owners will keep their own tools and decide use in terms of their own priorities.
4. The group would compensate for equipment use with credit which could be applied to labor or the use of other equipment.
5. The group would assume some share of the costs for the repair and depreciation of the equipment it used.

In order to determine the extent of available equipment, Susie suggested that everyone fill out an information card. Skills, experience, chores to be rotated, needs, hours available, as well as tools could then be filed for group use.

```
FILE CARD
NAME:
PHONE:
ADDRESS:
SKILLS:
TOOLS:
CHORE ROTATION:
NEEDS:
HOURS:
```

Your group might want to go further than Ken and Susie's and create a communally supplied and centrally located workshop or garden or darkroom, kitchen or laundry, auto mechanic garage or screening room. Rotating-use charts and group maintenance and insurance fees would promote the smooth functioning of these facilities.

The people in Susie and Ken's barter group believed in the development of an emotional support system. They decided that psychological and emotional needs and skills could be traded as readily as more tangible goods and services.

In order to do this, they established a rotating "hot line" emergency system. A person would always be available to respond to emotional crises. They also agreed that half of their business meetings would be spent in honest personal discussion about the nonmaterial issues—such as health, career, friendship, sexuality, politics—that affected their lives. If people had certain skills which could help someone in need, they would receive labor credits for the time spent helping. Ken, for instance, was terribly upset about lack of tenure. This made him tense and unable to concentrate on the book he was writing. By admitting it openly during one of the meetings, he was able to get help from a member who knew a variety of relaxation techniques. This help was "credited" as though it were any other skilled labor job.

Once your barter group has a secure base and operates smoothly, all your friends are going to want to join! *Do not let the size of the group get too unwieldy.* Instead, help them start their own barter groups. A few barter clusters in your city can be the beginning of a real economic transformation in your lives. Through networking and shared distribution or transportation systems, your group, in cooperation with the other groups, can develop a viable economic alternative that eschews profit and remains responsive to the material and nonmaterial needs of its participants.

A successful neighborhood barter group will also provoke the interest of the community around it. This visibility gives you the opportunity to reach out to others in your area and draw them into the bartering structure. Your group provides a base from which you can encourage people to question political and economic assumptions about our society. In large part, your success is an answer to the question, can anything be done?

Community involvement might lead you into another area altogether—organizing a major nonprofit barter institution whose primary purpose is to affect the social and economic conditions of large groups of people.

LARGE-SCALE EXCHANGE

A large-scale, nonprofit, incorporated exchange has a broad-based membership drawing on a wide variety of resources, goods, and services. It possesses advantages you might want to consider.

More individuals and small businesses participate in an economic structure valuing personal connection and personal control. The wider variety of goods and services in the bartering pool enables you to trade for things not possible on a more limited level. Greater flexibility in terms of credit and debit means you can plan certain jobs for barter, space them during the year, and not have to depend so much on an item's immediate availability.

Moreover, by starting a nonprofit exchange you reach people who really benefit by this economic alternative—the unemployed, elderly, welfare recipients, students, farmworkers. Involving the economically disenfranchised not only gives you access to federal program money (which you may or may not want to take), foundation support, and local industry tax write-offs, but gives you across-the-board opportunity to start the process of social change.

There are different kinds of nonprofit exchanges. Some are geared to meet specific social needs; others are attached as nonprofit adjuncts to business corporations. Some limit their focus to members of a particular life style, whether it be spiritual, sexual, or political; others try to involve everyone. Some exist primarily on paper through newsletter networking; others go directly to community centers, churches, campuses, and unemployment offices and set up portable minioffices. Some get embroiled in social service agencies; others strive to stay clear of bureaucracy altogether.

Remember that this is not a project to be undertaken lightly. Unlike a neighborhood group, an exchange cannot be formed in off-hours, with casual coffee-klatch planning sessions. Nor can it rely on the goodwill of friends and the energy of group spirit for its survival. The more ragged edges there are to your organization, the easier it will be for it to unravel.

You must start an exchange in a businesslike way. And this means you have to *get funding, establish a board of directors, draw up articles of incorporation* and *democratic bylaws, delineate responsibilities, set up a workable system for trading,* and then go out and *solicit members.*

LARGE-SCALE BARTER GROUP

The Service Exchange in Portland, Oregon, can be used as an example of how one group evolved.

It was started by Wayne Mayo, a concerned citizen, who felt that a service exchange would help the unemployed make their money last longer.

He went to his church and presented his idea to its board of directors. He wanted to establish a way for the unemployed to employ themselves on a nonmonetary basis. He also wanted to integrate the skills of professionals, so that first-rate health and legal care would be available to those who otherwise could not afford it. Mayo wanted to start a large-scale, heterogeneous service exchange.

The board thought his idea promising and provided him with a solid core of advisers: a lawyer, a marketing expert, a retired manager of a social service agency, and an accountant.

Mayo researched his idea according to specific suggestions made by his advisers. He held a meeting of interested participants and backers. He familiarized himself with laws regulating nonprofit corporations and, with the lawyer's help, became incorporated. From his small but secure base of church members and volunteer labor, Mayo began a city-wide membership and fund-raising drive.

Because of its nonprofit status, the Service Exchange had access to public service time on radio and television. Mayo put together quality spots that explained the dynamics of barter within the context of the exchange.

The response was quite rewarding. However, each new member was told that the exchange was in the process of *forming* a resource file; that patience was necessary; that individual needs probably could not be met until the list of resources had grown. By establishing realistic expectations, Mayo cut down negative feelings and dissatisfied participants.

Mayo claims that the Service Exchange now matches, on the average, 50 to 60 percent of the requests it receives; moreover, once people get the hang of it, they start bartering on their own. Unlike profit barter club owners, Mayo is delighted about this. It is exactly what he had in mind when meditating on the meaning of "salt of the earth."

Getting funds is always difficult when you begin; people are skeptical about supporting you. Mayo attacked the problem on a number of fronts.

He sent letters to the foundations of local industry, outlining the nature of his exchange, why it was beneficial to individuals and to the community. He used specific examples to illustrate each point. He explained the exchange's financial situation and requested an exact amount from each local foundation. The request always equaled 5 percent of the total budget, never a penny more. He assured each foundation that he was *depending* on a donation of that sum, and with few exceptions he received the contribution.

Mayo also applied for and received CETA (Comprehensive Employment Training Act) funds. These were funneled through the city's federal revenue-sharing programs. Before receiving this money, Mayo and the others had been working on a volunteer basis. They were now able to hire previously unemployed people to staff their tiny office and to answer their elaborate phone setup.

Because CETA money is based on the rate of unemployment in the local area, it is not a stable money source. If unemployment goes down, CETA funds are withdrawn. Mayo has begun the arduous process of applying for a federal pilot project grant. Unlike other groups, his does not charge membership dues or request pledges payable either in cash or service, but these are certainly viable options for your group.

Mayo attributes the success of the Service Exchange to at least three key factors: (1) He did not promise more than he could deliver, (2) The church gave him a membership core that provided his starting base, and (3) He had experts (marketing, legal, financial) guiding him all the way.

ORGANIZATIONAL STEPS

You don't need the entire board of a church at your disposal. But before you begin, establish a survey committee. Even if it is only a committee of one—you—this is a necessary first step!

The survey committee must search out all the facts so people can properly assess feasibility and decide for themselves whether or not they want ot commit time, energy, and money to your barter group. The survey committee must have accurate information about the following:

1. Need
2. Potential membership
3. Estimates of transaction volume
4. Management skills needed
5. Facilities needed
6. Operating costs
7. Capitalization

Once you here detailed information and realistic organizational plans for each of these categories, then have a meeting and invite everyone you can think of who might be interested.

The enthusiastic potential members will want to set up an organizing committee. Do not be a martyr. Do not refuse help. The only way to establish a large-scale barter club is with the aid of others. Inherent in the concept of such a club is reciprocity, labor exchange, mutual aid, and shared responsibility.

Accept the participation of an organizing committee, whose purpose is to:

1. Sign up the required number of members
2. Obtain capital
3. Draft the legal organization papers
4. File articles of incoroporation
5. Arrange the first *official* meeting at which the articles of incorporation and bylaws are adopted, a responsible board of directors is elected, and arrangements are made for banking, bookkeeping, persons authorized to handle funds and issue checks, and all the other details presented by the survey committee are resolved

Start out with conservative, realistic expectations.

One realistic expectation is that your club will be set up in such a way that the profiteering and chicanery of the more disreputable barter clubs do *not* take place. This will be possible because, unlike the private business exchanges, your club will be set up along democratic principles. Officers will be elected from the membership at large. They will occupy limited terms of office. You will vote by secret ballot. Your records will be open. Your monthly meetings will provide everyone with the opportunity to air complaints and voice suspicions.

A second realistic expectation is that you will organize your exchange in an efficient manner. Trading will be facilitated, not hindered. Management will be enthusiastic.

It is important to hire a good office manager, to pay the manager a good salary, and to let the manager manage!

REFERRAL SYSTEMS

Barter groups also have referral systems which work. The systems themselves, however, vary from group to group.

Wayne Mayo's Service Exchange does not operate as a labor bank. It does not keep track of people's credits and debits. All exchanges are direct. Mayo feels that with a membership of 3,000 to 5,000, a banking system would be too impersonal. Instead, there is a complicated filing system which, declares Mayo, works well.

It is organized in the following manner. In a small office, two full-time and three part-time people (fifteen to twenty hours per week) handle two phones equipped with three-way calling systems, a call-forwarding service, and a call-waiting service. The filing is done in a series of flat Rolodexes, each specifying a different category.

The category is based on what people do. One file, for example, is titled Construction. This contains cards with the following subdivisions: blacktoppers, carpenters, roofers. Under the subdivisions, different colored tags indicate the part of town where people live. Under the colored tags is a list of the people, their zip code, and phone number. A prefix indicates where the person lives in relation to the person calling with the need for the service.

CATEGORY: construction

SUBHEADING: roofer

COLOR TAG: X section of town

ZIP CODE AND PHONE PREFIX: Y neighborhood

In the master file, all the members are listed in alphabetical order. Pertinent information about each person, such as special skills or interests, as well as the main skills, is included, as are the person's service needs. (This latter data is written in pencil as it is subject to periodic change.)

> MASTER FILE
> NAME:
> SKILL:
> ADDITIONAL SKILLS:
> NEEDS:

After consulting the filing system to match needs, a three-way call is made. Mayo was afraid that people would be shy about calling each other directly, so the Service Exchange provides the introductory phone call and helps begin the negotiating process for the parties involved. After this first phone conversation, further transactions are left in the hands of the barterers.

The Community Energy Bank in Eugene, Oregon, is organized differently. Exchanges occur in the following ways:

1. Trading between individuals, one to one, without the use of the credit-hour system
2. Using the credit hours recorded in the Energy Bank filing system
3. Combining credit hours and money
4. Offering an item in trade for other items, for credit hours, or for money

The instruction sheet specifies that all contracts be made prior to work done and that at the completion of a job, all members comment on supplied forms. (This is a way of eliminating irresponsible members.) The index system consists of the following three categories:

1. A membership file, where members gets their corresponding number, list all their experience, tools, assets, credentials, and needs
2. Services-offered file, listing by category and subject members who offer skills, etc.
3. Services-needed file, listing by category and subject members who need skills, etc.

NETWORKS

Another way of distributing barter information is through newsletters, directories, and public service time on radio and television. This form of distribution shifts all responsibility for making contact and for negotiating deals to the individuals involved.

It does not work well for members unaccustomed to taking initiative, nor for those who may feel uncomfortable dealing with new situations. But the use of the media for information distribution is quite effective on a statewide level, and absolutely necessary in setting up networks connecting people, clusters of groups, or geographical areas.

Self-Determination, a California statewide network, eliminated automated information and retrieval systems, switchboard crisis units, and other systems of organization in favor of a directory, augmented by supported services. As Gloria Rose Ott explains, "The reasons for the choice were multiple: a directory is convenient to use and can be shared among working or study groups; it is a proven form, both economically feasible and capable of maximizing descriptive communications."

Anne Dosher, cofounder of San Diego's Community Congress Network, prescribes the following guidelines to any network organization:

1. State your purpose and articulate long- and short-range goals.
2. Face power issues openly and quickly.
3. Share credit. Establish interdependence as the interactive model.
4. Give priority to information processing.
5. Keep membership diverse. Include people with skills in facilitating group dynamics, interpersonal communicating, conceptualizing, planning, and mobilizing the change process.
6. Think of the network as a learning system.
7. Maintain lines of accountability, responsibility, and negotiability.
8. Evaluate the network stringently, with solid measuring devices.
9. Keep good records.

By adhering to these guidelines, the Community Congress not only is able to celebrate "the economies of love," and acquire "new meanings for ways of being in the world," but has also acquired millions of dollars for alternative human service agencies, confronted community issues, nurtured new agencies, obtained training grants, changed the relation between funding organizations and their funded institutions, and improved the structures for decision-making processes on local governmental level.

Let us return to *your* barter club.

Where are you now?

You have studied the laws of incorporation, small businesses, and nonprofit institutions. These are available from the secretary of state and the corporation commissioners.

You have figured out your budget and provided for capitalization either through private donations, public funding, grants, or dues.

You have decided whether your club's main function is

to act as a clearinghouse for information or to establish exchange terms and operate along banking credit-debit principles.

In either case, you have an office and you have set up a system of information distribution which enables members to barter skills, services, or goods. Assuming you do not have access to computers or elaborate automated devices, you have done this with filing cards and indexes, some sort of phone system, newsletters, or a directory.

You have solicited membership, democratically elected your officers, hired a manager. You are ready to roll.

Congratulations! You are on your way to proving that barter is better. Not only are you winning the fight against inflation and high taxes, but you are creating a new and viable economic structure that validates the best, instead of the worst, in its participants and their community.

9.

One Barter Family: How They Live

Molly is a weaver and, after an absence, has returned to college. Taylor is a college-educated garage mechanic. They live, with their three children, in Tucson, Arizona. Now in their mid-thirties, Molly and Taylor met over fifteen years ago, when they were living in Greenwich Village and working as coffeehouse managers at such places as The Fat Black Pussy Cat and the Why Not?

Molly does not look like she is from the Village. She is a redheaded Southerner by birth and blood. She lived in the South before her mother took her to New York. But when she speaks, it is in New York rhythms, fast and smart, with an apologetic laugh for being so much cleverer than you might expect.

Taylor grew up on a Mormon farm in Utah, where he learned the basic mechanical skills that were to serve him once he took up bartering. Although he had always rebuilt his own engines and done his own tune-ups, after college Taylor thought of himself strictly as a white-collar executive with clean fingernails and a BA in philosophy.

During their Village years, Molly and Taylor had spent much time together. But they began to grow tired of New

York City and, after a while, they went their separate ways.

Molly married, had a baby, and then spent a number of years traveling around the country, bartering her services—as baby-sitter, cashier, copyeditor and cartoonist—for room and board. When she learned how to weave, her bartering increased and she began exchanging weavings for books, records, health care, and other people's art.

Taylor, meanwhile, had moved to Tucson with his family. He was leading a much more conventional life, doing graduate work in Chinese philosophy.

In one of those strange quirks of fate, Molly passed through Tucson for the first time in years just after Taylor's wife had left for California, leaving him with two young daughters (Caren, now nine, and Elise, ten) and without her $7,000-a-year salary. Taylor was in the midst of what he calls his "minibreakdown," during which he grew to find his job as a social worker for the state of Arizona intolerable, and quit. When he met Molly for the second time, the $14,000-a-year income to which he was accustomed had shrunk to less than $3,000.

During this period, Molly gave him a great deal of emotional support. They fell in love, and after a time, she and her daughter, Tamaya (now eleven), moved into the rustic little house he owned in Pueblo Gardens.

Pueblo Gardens, a lower-middle-class FHA development on the south side, is one of the few integrated neighborhoods in Tucson. Blacks, Chicanos, white Southerners, truckers, miners, and Midwestern retirees live on streets named Barleycorn, Amigo, and McFee. Molly and Taylor's house is the only one on the block that is not afraid to stand out like a sore thumb. A cheerfully colored children's playhouse made of wooden doors and old tires, a rope and ladder climbing structure, and an antiquated Chevrolet converted to a play car give the patina of antiestablishment funk in the midst of blue-collar propriety.

After quitting his job as a social worker, Taylor rediscovered his joy in working with his hands, both as a wooden tool carver and as a mechanic, and he gave up white-collar work permanently. Now, as he slides under cars in his garage, sticking his bearded head out to ask for a wrench, he looks nothing like the unhappy social worker he once was.

Moreover, aided by Molly's enthusiastic skill as a barterer, Taylor has developed an entirely new attitude toward money.

Last year, the combined cash income for both Molly and Taylor was less than $5,000. It scarcely seems possible that a family of five can survive on that. And yet, they not only managed to survive, but to survive in comfort. Because some regular monthly payments in cash are necessary, they try to maintain an income that consists of one-third cash to two-thirds barter. Their $4,500 in cash income last year was augmented by an equivalent of $9,000 in barter. With the exception of utility bills, phone bills, insurance premiums, mortgage payments, gasoline, and certain food purchases, barter paid for everything.

For them, barter makes the difference between voluntary simplicity and involuntary simplicity. In their words, it "lightens the heart and adds ease and grace" to their lives.

How do they do it? What are the rhythms, the patterns created by barter?

Barter moves both by design and by accident. Molly and Taylor delight in the serendipitous—like the time when an organic-food delivery truck broke down near Taylor's garage and the owner didn't have enough money for repairs. He remembered Taylor's ad on the food co-op bulletin board, "Fix Cars—Will Barter." In exchange for repairing the truck, Taylor received organic groceries for several weeks.

But fortuitous events aren't the only source of barter. Barter must work on a day-to-day basis as well. Let's follow Molly, Taylor, and the children through a week in their lives in order to see when and how barter works best.

MONDAY

7:30 A.M. Taylor wakes the girls, who are sleeping on the loft he and Molly built to give them extra play space underneath. The toys in their room were gifts from grandparents, but the furniture, like that in the rest of the house, was purchased at second-hand stores, garage sales, swap meets, or else left by friends, bartered, or found. It is simple but imaginative.

The most expensive item in the house (paid for in cash) is Molly's four-harness loom, which she bought at a crafts fair for $100 and could sell today for $1,000. The second most expensive item is the $20 reclining chair that came from Goodwill. The signed Tiffany lamp Taylor found hangs above a slightly worn but lovely bartered Chinese rug. An old steamer trunk has been put to new use as a chest of drawers. Lamps, trunks, bureaus, tables, chairs, and mirrors are each of a distinct and particular vintage, overlapped within small space like a three-dimensional collage.

The girls dress. Their clothes come from Goodwill and from weaving students who sew them as payment for lessons from Molly. Breakfast, a superhealthy meal of seven-grain cereal, comes from the barter with the organic-food supplier who needed truck repairs.

9:00 A.M. Caren, Elise, and Tamaya go to a public alternative school in which the guiding principle is that learning occurs through experience. The children's schoolrooms have been converted into a town, featuring houses, stores, and streets made entirely by the students. In this town the students have their own government, print their own scrip, and learn the rudiments of market economy by creating one of their own.

Barter is a dominant factor in their play economy. Not only were building materials feverishly traded (cardboard for linoleum tiles for fabric for glue), but the student shopkeepers trade their own products with each other instead of using scrip because, say the children, the scrip is too inflated. Value for value, cinnamon toothpicks for banana cake is a better deal.

The girls walk in. They go to a friend's "store" and discover a bonanza. Her mother supplies tennis shoes to supermarkets. She has donated the seconds to her daughter's shop.

Caren quickly goes into action. She brings out fistfuls of scrip and buys a pair of red sneakers. Elise and Tamaya aren't so quick to act—they are out of scrip.

First Elise convinces Caren to give her some. "I'll do the dishes for you for a whole week!" Then Tamaya negotiates a deal with her friend. She will help sell merchandise in exchange for shoes of her choice.

Within minutes, the three girls sport brand new tennis shoes! Then it is time for more structured classes to begin.

12:00 NOON. After spending the morning writing a sociology paper on her last year's experience as coordinator of Tucson's Free University, Molly grabs a quick lunch at a sandwich shop. It is free because she did the calligraphy on the menus.

She then drives to the office of Free University, where she volunteers her services on Monday mornings. The Free University is housed neared the University of Arizona campus. She escapes from the intense desert heat into the air-conditioned cool and settles down to help with registration.

Free U, as it is called, is an off-campus organization that offers nonaccredited courses ranging from gestalt therapy techniques to desert natural history. The minimal fees are payable either in cash or barter. The connection with Free U is vital for Molly and her family. It puts them in touch with an entire community of people willing to barter.

The students range from teen-agers to senior citizens. Some have already bartered their $5 registration fees and are painting the Free U office. Molly checks through the cards. She notices that a Dr. Cohen, an optometrist, has signed up for aquarium biology and thinks of the trouble with her glasses she has been having recently and the headaches she has gotten because of it. She writes down Dr. Cohen's phone number. Then she examines the rest of the cards, noting how many have signed up for her weaving class and Taylor's auto repair class.

When she first started teaching weaving at Free U, Taylor's financial state was in shambles. He had middle-class debts he could not begin to pay off. He did not even have enough money to hire a lawyer and declare bankruptcy.

Then a lawyer's wife enrolled in Molly's weaving class and volunteered her husband's services in barter. "It was like a gift from heaven," Molly recalls. He made it possible for them to straighten out their financial affairs so that they did not have to declare bankruptcy.

Since then, their finances have been fine. "Taylor threw out his charge cards and keeping a budget is a mutual effort," says Molly. "And we have found that *literally* because of trading, we don't feel the pinch the way to we used to."

5:00 P.M. Taylor's garage, Funky Motors. On most days, Taylor is here from 9:00 A.M. until 6:00 P.M. Located in the oldest garage–gas station in Tucson, an art deco building of thick adobe walls, Taylor's small operation services friends, university personnel, students, and barterers of all varieties. His income is about half cash, half barter. His barter arrangement with the landlady includes rent and the use of tools and equipment, in exchange for tuning the cars she brings him.

Taylor struggles with an orange ten-speed bike—a barter job. Finished, he turns to work on a VW engine—cash customer. Taylor works on a first-come, first-serve basis.

"I don't set aside trade work for cash work, even though I might need the cash more, because I see no difference in my obligation to do the job. I am fighting against the attitude that time is money. Barter is one way to do it."

A '74 Cutlass rattles up. Inside, Ellen, a twenty-three-year-old friend, waves. She is working on her MA in audiology at the University of Arizona and she is broke. Her car needs front shocks, front brakes, and an oil change. She is eager to barter, but has no idea what she can offer in exchange.

"Hah!" exclaims Taylor, thinking of the ornately carved piano which has been sitting unplayed since he and Molly bartered for it. "Teach piano, that's what you can do."

A prodigy in her Brooklyn neighborhood at the age of four, Ellen had studied piano until she was eighteen. She is good with the children and has the time. Taylor explains she will have to pay for parts. He only barters labor. They are both pleased, and agree on the exchange.

7:00 P.M. Dinner. Molly fixes more healthy bartered food —brown rice, vegetable casserole, fruit salad, and kefir to drink. The children do their homework and go to bed, Molly and Taylor, science fiction buffs, read paperbacks that they traded at a two-for-one paperback store.

11:00 P.M. Bed.

TUESDAY

10:30 A.M. Molly calls Dr. Cohen from her home phone. (Phone bills, like all utilities, are paid in cash.) Yes, he is open to barter! He does not want weavings, but he certainly can use auto repair. His sixteen-year-old daughter's Karmen Ghia always need fixing. At the moment, the clutch cable is broken and the front headlight is smashed. They set up appointments for eye examinations for Molly, Taylor, and

Tamaya. Molly is relieved that her headaches will come to an end.

She now calls a list of dentists, hoping one of them will be as receptive to barter. "Once you have bartered with one professional," she has learned, "others are more likely to grant you credibility." She uses their lawyer's name as a reference, mentioning Dr. Cohen for good measure.

1:00 P.M. At the garage, John, a potter, drops by to see Taylor. He has designed a peddle-power potter's wheel and wants Taylor to go over the mechanical drawings. In exchange, he will give Taylor some pottery. Taylor does not need pottery, but John is a friend. "It is hard to say no to a barter when it is someone you trust and there are no hassles involved." He goes over the drawings at lunch—hamburger and French fries, paid for in cash.

3:00 P.M. The children find a kitten on their way home from school. They plead with Molly to let them keep it. She points out they have two cats and a dog already. Finally, unable to resist the kitten herself, she makes a deal—the children have to make their beds and do all the dishes without being reminded. They agree and promptly name their new pet Whiskers.

8:00 P.M. Having spent the day unsuccessfully trying to find a dentist who will barter, Molly is doubly disappointed that none signed up for her weaving class that night. The class meets in a rent-free room, donated as a public service by one of the local banks. She has twelve students of all ages. She looks around the group and assesses different barter possibilities.

"I feel a responsibility when I say in my classes I am open to barter, that I don't just limit it to experienced barterers. So many people are terrified the first time. I don't want to prove them right. When I barter with first-timers I tend to be more flexible. And I'll give them advice. 'Relax. We'll work something out. Don't sell yourself short. Your time is worth more than that.' I'll suggest things for them to barter and when they deliver, I'll really praise them. I believe in barter and in Free U. If it weren't for barter, there would be no point to Free U. It would be just like any other institution."

One student has the idea of doing laundry. Molly considers this a boon. She helps the student dicker. "Ask how much work is involved," she prompts.

"How much?"

"About three big baskets a week," Molly answers.

'Does it need to be sorted?"

"Yes."

"How much do you want me to do?"

"All of it."

The student looks worried. "I don't know if I have the time."

"How much do you have time for?"

The student hesitates. Molly doesn't press.

"Why don't you think about it and tell me next class."

Molly believes it is essential to know what your time and energy are worth to you *before* you begin dickering in a barter. Moreover, you have to pay close attention to your feelings. If you feel tense, uptight, and pushed, tell the other person. From past experience, Molly has learned to stay clear of barters which are not mutually satisfactory. At the end of a barter negotiation, she always asks if the other person thinks it is a fair trade and she listens carefully to the answer. "There is nothing worse than having someone in your life who feels he's gotten the worst end of a deal."

Barters from this semester's weaving class include sewing lessons, fresh baked cakes, and ballet classes for Caren, who has been wanting to learn to dance.

WEDNESDAY

9:00 A.M. The children go to school and Molly goes to junior college, where she will finish the year and then apply to the University of Arizona. The level of Molly's work in freshman composition was so high that her English teacher worked out an arrangement with her. She would be his unacknowledged teaching assistant and help him correct papers, while he would give her credit for two classes instead of one, as well as privately supervising her writing.

11:00 A.M. Taylor takes an hour off from the garage and goes to the silversmith cooperative on Fourth Avenue. One of the jewelers owes him $50 worth of jewelry for auto repairs. He decides to use part of the credit for some exquisite turquoise and silver earrings—a sixtieth-birthday present for Molly's mother.

The silversmith cooperative exemplifies an alternative life style subculture in Tucson. Items dealing with spiritual and creative energies as well as business particulars are written into its corporate bylaws. Many of the coop's members came from large cities in other states in the mid-1960s, where they had led conventional lives. At that point, they gave up their careers as advertising executives, middle-class housewives, and high school teachers, began learning new skills, and with their families, came to Tucson to live and work.

They barter as a matter of course, often initiating trades with their customers. They insure cash remuneration for cost of materials plus a certain percentage extra needed to keep the store running.

6:30 P.M. That night, when Molly comes home from school and Taylor from work, they are angry at the girls for not doing their chores. A family conference is held before dinner. Barter is the operative metaphor. Molly tries to get the girls to understand.

"Not only have you not upheld your end of the bargain we made about the kitten, but just in general, when you look at our lives together, we're making a trade. Daddy's doing things for you. I'm doing things for you. You have to hold your end up. If you don't hold your end up, why should we hold up ours? A family is an economic unit. Time and energy are worth something. You have to understand that."

Embarrassed, the girls clean up while Taylor cooks spaghetti (from the food coop) and Molly makes a salad with fresh greens from the produce barter.

8:00 P.M. Ellen comes over to give Elise her first piano lesson. Taylor is surprised that Ellen came so soon. Usually there is more of a lag between making a deal and carrying it out.

Barter time is slower than dollar time. A transaction is seldom immediate, observes Taylor. You spend time getting to know the other person. Often you make a deal for something to happen in the future. You take that risk because you trust the other person. You trust the other person because you've spent time together.

This is one of the reasons Molly enjoys barter. "I like to digest things at my own rate. With barter, I'm never in a time crunch. It's relaxing."

THURSDAY

8:00 A.M. The girls are dressed, the beds are made, and a breakfast of bartered eggs and cash-purchased sausages is on the table.

11:00 A.M. Molly visits the Fourth Avenue Merchants Association. Every year it sponsors a fair to which artisans bring their crafts. The fair is one of the few public places where Molly can display weavings and foster new contacts for barter. She does not want to pay the $45 fee plus the $17.50 in booth rental, however, so she goes to the Merchants Association in order to work out a trade.

She is successful. Instead of paying fees in cash, she will be able to donate one of her weavings as a prize for the Merchant Association raffle that traditionally ends the fair.

1:00 P.M. At the alternative school, a little girl comes up to Caren and wants to trade for a stick of gum.

"What do you have?" asks Caren.

"A stuffed animal. It's brand new," replies the little girl. Caren loves stuffed animals and looks at the furry monkey longingly, but she shakes her head and hands the girl a stick of gum.

"That's not a fair trade. You can have the gum free."

She walks into the art class where she will learn how to sew a sleeping bag for the little crocheted mouse Molly had made her. Her sister is there, weaving.

"What a stupid girl," she tells her sister. "She was going to trade a stuffed animal for a stick of gum!"

4:00 P.M. Molly has spent the day weaving. Now she takes the girls to the backpacking store, where they have a barter credit. Although they don't backpack, they do camp, especially when they visit Taylor's parents in Utah. They select some cooking utensils and a daypack for the girls to share.

6:00 P.M. Dinner. Chores. Homework.

8:00 P.M. Taylor's Free U auto-repair class is a popular one. It meets in his garage, so that he can demonstrate the equipment. This term most of his students pay him cash. But one woman barters meat, and a young man offers potted plants. Taylor's former therapist, with whom he had traded auto work for therapy, is present.

"I've decided to start fixing my own car," he says, handing Taylor the fee in cash.

It used to be that Taylor and Molly had some months when there was an abundance of services, but not enough money for mortgage payments. It was the single major source of their financial anxiety. With experience, they have learned to maintain their best ratio between cash and barter, and not to accept more barter than they can handle. Taylor is not at all unhappy about being paid in dollars for his class.

FRIDAY

8:30 A.M. The girls remember that today is zoo day. All the children will bring animals to school and make a zoo for their "town." Whiskers, their new kitten, is chosen.

Molly gets a call before she takes them to school. The weaving student has decided to do the laundry. This pleases Molly, who hates doing laundry and keeps postponing it.

After she drops the children off, she heads to her junior college.

9:30 A.M. Taylor is at the garage. As a rule, he divides his barters into ordinary trades and class operations. "Class" refers to barters such as the one with the optometrist, in which $250 to $300 worth of fees will be paid through auto repair. "Ordinary" refers to the day-to-day trading that goes on for car parts, tires, yard work, house repairs.

Today Taylor negotiates an ordinary barter with a transmission fluid supplier. The supplier had been attracted by Taylor's brand-new off-beat sign, "Funky Motors." (The sign was a barter for hauling a friend's trash to the dump in his pickup truck.)

Taylor's appeal to alternate life stylers is deliberate. When he first got to Tucson, "as a stranger, it was easier getting into the alternate life style and I liked what was happening. I liked the various aspects I saw—the spiritual, the communal, the sharing, the volunteering in social services. If something was needed and useful to society, these people didn't wait for the government to do it. They did it themselves. They weren't rioting. They were working for change."

Barter fit into the questioning of a money economy. It

was something the government could not touch. It was an aspect of the alternate life style with which Taylor felt comfortable.

The transmission fluid supplier admires the interior of Taylor's garage. It's walls are chalk white. The yin and yang symbol is painted in bright orange. Though he has quit academic studies in Chinese philosophy, Taoism remains an important influence in Taylor's thought.

He sees anarchism as part of its appeal. "I want to be left alone. Anarchism says I can be left alone. Taoism says I should be left alone." The concept that the government which governs least is best is inherent in Tao. The fewer regulations there are, the more people will behave in a natural, and therefore ideal, way. Taylor links this to barter.

"Any way that you get around money, which is a basis of governmental power and control, you are living a more Taoist life. The more you are able to trade your own skills directly without the intermediary of money, the closer you are to reaching a society without government."

3:30 P.M. On her way home from school, Molly stops at Buffalo Exchange, a used clothing store that takes clothes in trade. She drops off skirts she no longer wants and uses the credit for a pair of Levis and some T-shirts.

7:00 P.M. The family eats a credit dinner at a small friendly restaurant that features one of Molly's weavings on the wall. The children regale their parents with the wild escapades of Whiskers and Speedy, a desert tortoise, who managed to disrupt the zoo.

After dinner they all go to a free film classic shown by the campus film society.

SATURDAY

10:00 A.M. Elise, who handles wrenches like a grease monkey and loves to help her father, accompanies him to the garage. The weaving student comes over to do the laundry. Caren and Tamaya ride their new garage-sale bikes to visit friends. Molly makes a niçoise salad to take to her friend Angie's wedding reception and finishes off the particularly lovely weaving she has been making as a gift.

She watches the pile of clean, folded laundry grow. "It's a luxury barter, I know. But we can afford it right now. If money were really tight, I'd do it myself and let the student do a different barter." When you have the money to pay the bills, explains Molly, but not enough for the frivolities, barter makes life more pleasant.

"When I grew up, we really didn't have a lot of money to spare. There was enough for necessities, of course, but not a lot left over for movies, roller skating or bicycles. Our kids would be living some version of that life if it weren't for the trading we do. Because of barter, birthdays and holidays are special for them. They get presents they really want. And, in between, they get piano lessons, ballet lessons, books, records, art supplies. In terms of our cash income, we're poor. But the nice thing is that with barter we never feel that way—we always feel we have enough."

2:00 P.M. Angie and Carlos's wedding is an informal one, with food cooked by friends and dancing on the lawn. Carlos is a beekeeper and owns a ranch out in the country. He trades honey for most of the simple necessities of his life. Angie, on the other hand, is a city woman. The ranch will be a new experience for her.

9:00 P.M. Caren is engaged in a hot game of dominoes with her barter baby-sitter, Alexander, whose motorcycle Taylor repaired after a mild accident. Caren's two sisters are sleeping at the homes of friends, and her parents have gone to hear bluegrass music at a club. Because of their barter arrangements with the owners, Molly and Taylor never pay a cover charge and drinks are on the house.

SUNDAY

10:00 A.M. Taylor makes a delicious breakfast of freshly squeezed orange juice (from the orange tree) and pancakes made of bartered stone-ground flour. Their year's supply of honey was a trade with Carlos for tractor repairs.

The girls are deep into their game of Monopoly. Molly sips coffee and listens to Taylor play the alto recorder she bartered for him at a music store last Christmas.

Suddenly, Taylor stops. He remembers he'd told his friend John, the potter, that they would come and visit.

The kids, the dog, Molly, and Taylor pile into the bright blue pickup truck (bartered for a van) and head to the outskirts of Tucson. Once past Mission San Xavier, glowing white and grand in the distance, the desert reasserts itself. Tumbleweed inexplicably starts and stops its perennial journey while lizards eye it with infinite stillness. Tucson schedules are forgotten. Time gentles into rhythms much more to Taylor's and Molly's liking.

They approach the house, a low adobe structure graced by an olive tree. John is in the patio working clay. His wife, Glenda, is a tanned fifty-year-old woman who has returned to graduate school in anthropology. But she still makes lovely porcelain pots, and she barters them. She is now firing ceramic pieces in the kiln. Two peddle-powered potter's wheels have been assembled under the palm-frond ramada. Curious conglomerations of bicycle wheels and "readily available parts" are John's solution to the energy crisis.

"Any good scrounger can make these for under $100," he explains to Molly. "I sell the booklet with instructions for assembly."

Taylor approves the changes in the mechanical drawings. John tells him to select a ceramic piece. The kids immerse themselves in a bucket of clay. Molly falls in love with two porcelain bowls and a large café au lait mug. Taylor's barter with John only covers the mug. She has to arrange a further trade.

Molly loves to have beautiful things, but rarely barters for them. Since her major economic contribution to the family is through barter, she feels guilty if what she gets does not benefit everyone. However, she wants the porcelain bowls enough to overcome her usual reluctance.

Glenda is not sure about a weaving, but Molly suggests they could design one together.

"In fact," she says, "I would love to do a big one for you in exchange for a set of new dinner dishes."

"That might be nice," responds Glenda. "I'll come by and look at yarns and things. We'll work something out. In the meantime, take the bowls and at least we'll get the barter started."

Molly is pleased. "It used to be that I couldn't do that—walk away from a barter with my end half-finished. It felt like stealing. I'm much more confident about the process's completing itself now."

4:00 P.M. The girls finish their clay sculptures. Molly wraps her bowls and cup. Taylor declines the offer of fresh goat's milk, which John gets in exchange for milking a neighbor's goat. They drive off, the silhouette of the olive tree receding in the sunset.

6:00 P.M. Molly uses her new bowls when she serves dinner. Elise practices the piano. Taylor watches television (a bartered set, of course). Tamaya goes to her room to write a book report. Caren plays with Whiskers.

The week has come to a close.

Molly and Taylor are comfortable with the considerable role barter plays in their lives. Their use of barter in Tucson is fairly well structured. They belong to institutions such as Free U, which gives barter a stable base and a useful predictability. They are friends with people who like to trade. They seek out those exchanges which benefit their family as a whole; which fulfill, in large measure, their responsibility as parents.

Barter doesn't work smoothly 100 percent of the time. There are frustrations and disappointments. Sometimes, as with the dentist, it takes too long. Other times, they are short of cash because they have overbartered. But for the most part, barter accomplishes for Molly and Taylor what they want—integration of economics with people, life style, and social values.

It did not happen immediately. They had to learn to trust the process.

"We got used to the fact that barter was really a good thing to do," says Molly. "We watched people who did it a lot and learned by their example. We kept doing it. We kept getting more and more confidence. Now we don't wait for anyone to suggest a barter. We always ask. They can only turn us down!"

With practice comes knowledge. Here is Molly and Taylor's list of helpful things to know when you barter:

1. Unlike bargaining, you can't act indifferent. You have to show interest. But don't act overanxious or overhesitant. Be relaxed and feel confident that everything will work out.
2. If you initiate the barter, you have to know exactly what you want, how much, and what it is worth to you.

Is it worth the dollar equivalency, if there is one? If there is no price tag, how much of your energy is it worth?

3. Then say, "I really like that. Do you barter?"

4. Ask what the other person wants. He or she will usually ask you what you do. Go through a list of things—sometimes you have to reach—until you find something that interests them.

5. Then start dickering. To be successful, you must appear relaxed, and be clear about how far you will go. Keep in touch with your feelings. If it is too much, say, "Why don't we think about this until tomorrow."

6. At the end, ask the person how he or she feels about the result.

7. If you have been approached for a barter, make it clear whether or not you are open to it. Be specific about what you will take, although you can get wonderful things by listening to what others have to offer. Sometimes the lead will shift in a barter four or five times as to who wants what more, and pursues it most actively.

8. It's important not to hurt the other person by downgrading the value of their barter. It's not as though you're paying cash. It's a relationship. Small courtesies and consideration are crucial.

Appendix

BARTER ORGANIZATIONS
The following organizations either engage in barter or are
exploring decentralist economics which may include bartering. This list is by no means complete. It is intended to give
a random geographic sampling, and an organization's inclu-
sion does not necessarily imply the author's endorsement. The
reader is urged to inquire in his or her community as to other
organizations and, of course, to look carefully into the workings of any organization (whether listed or unlisted) before
joining.

NORTHEAST

BARTERTOWN
476 Broadway
New York, NY 10013
(212) 964-4190

BLACK TRUCK
36 Jay Street
Cambridge, MA 02139
(617) 491-0531
An anarchist collective that does trucking and moving. They bar-

ter and provide free services when needed for community, movement groups, and poor people.

CHANGE, INC.
381 Lafayette Street
New York, NY 10012

This international organization, which provides financial aid to artists, plans on donating $10 million worth of art to hospitals around the country. The hospitals that accept the donated art works agree to provide medical treatment to art professionals. The point is to insure medical care for poor artists. The program is underway in New York City at the Hospital for Joint Diseases and Jewish Hospital in Manhattan, LaGuardia Hospital and Medical Center in Brooklyn.

EVERYTHING FOR EVERYBODY
298 Columbus Avenue
Boston, MA
(617) 262-6634

This people's exchange service is a clearinghouse for sweat and inexpensive work as well as a perpetual free market. Membership is $5 a month or $100 for life. There are three New York locations as well.

INTERNATIONAL INDEPENDENCE INSTITUTE
Robert Swan
639 Massachusetts Avenue
Cambridge, MA 02139
(617) 661-4661

Works on a commodity-based currency, as successfully used in the Exeter experiment. Creative economic thinking goes on here.

PRINCETON CENTER FOR ALTERNATIVE FUTURES, INC.
60 Hodge Road
Princeton, NJ 08540
(609) 921-2280

"A deliberately small think tank and conference center for exploring alternative futures for industrialized countries in a planetary context of human interdependence." A good resource center for books written on economics that include bartering as a possible alternative.

VACATION EXCHANGE CLUB
350 Broadway
New York, NY 10013

Furnishes the Home Exchange Directory, which describes your

home and its particulars along with similar details of thousands
of other homes being offered for exchange during the year. Sub-
scription costs range from $9 to $15, depending on what time of
year and with which supplement you are getting the directory.
The directory contains more than 2,000 addresses from all over the
world.

SOUTH

CHARGE-A-TRADE
3081 East Commercial Blvd.
Fort Lauderdale, FL
(305) 491-2700

A business-oriented barter club that uses the credit-card system
and computers to keep track of exchanges.

COMMUNITY TECHNOLOGY/SOAP FACTORY
P.O. Box 32057
Washington, D.C. 20007
(202) 387-6933

A center for alternative businesses and community organizing. Barter is used when possible. Karl Hess was one of the founding spir-
its.

IMA CORPORATION/ABBA FOUNDATION
628 Frenchman Street
New Orleans, LA 70116
(504) 954-3340

A group of alternative businesses earn money to provide their
foundation with funds for community services. Many of the businesses are open to barter. In general, skills are more valued than
money.

INSTITUTE FOR LOCAL SELF-RELIANCE
1717 18th Street N.W.
Washington, D.C. 20009
(202) 232-4108

A good resource institute for information on alternative economics.
Membership costs $25 a year for individuals, $40 for institutions,
and includes subscriptions and a 20 percent discount on institute
publications.

QUAKER HOUSE
1384 Fairview Road N.E.
Atlanta, GA 30306
(404) 577-7986

A house where people can stay in exchange for donations of energy. The Quaker House is located in an alternative-life-style neighborhood where many of the people in the community trade skills and services, including restaurants which will trade food for your energy in helping out.

TRUE FEED EXCHANGE
Kent Whealy
R.F.D. 2 (MO)
Princeton, MO 64673

A nonprofit garden-feed exchange. Send one of your seeds plus stamps or $1 for the kind of seeds you want in exchange. A newsletter is available.

USEFUL SERVICES EXCHANGE
Reston, VA

Started in 1975 by Henry H. Ware, it now has 450 members. No registration fee. "A nonprofit community self-help program."

MIDWEST

BUSINESS OWNERS EXCHANGE
Minneapolis, MN

A business barter group with 329 members claiming to have turned over $1 million in trade in 1976. $150 joining fee and $25 a year in dues. Each member gets a $1,000 line of credit and routinely receives exchange checks when providing a product or service to another member. For purchases up to $150, members pay half in cash, half in exchange checks. For purchases over $150, the seller can demand 80 percent in cash. Buyers pay 7 percent a month interest on any money drawn from the line of credit.

COMMON GROUND CRISIS CENTER
1090 South Adams
Birmingham, MI 93130
(313) 645-9676

A face-to-face counseling center that is starting a people's yellow pages based on similar people's yellow pages all over the country. The center is also now gathering a list of talents and skills which will include barter, trade, or selling. The list of skills will sell for $1.

EMMA GOLDMAN CLINIC
715 North Dodge
Iowa City, IA
(319) 337-2111

A clinic which accepts barter, particularly in its Positive Experience Pregnancy Groups.

GROUP FOR COMMUNITY LEARNING
3240 Cleveland Avenue
Columbus, OH 43224

A group interested in creating a better sense of community. The group has had mixed experiences in starting neighborhood labor coops.

LEARNING EXCHANGE
Carol (Maura) Berk-Fonte
Ann Arbor, MI
(313) 599-1447

THE LEARNING EXCHANGE
P.O. Box 920
Evanston, IL 60204
(312) 273-3383

Trades close to 3,000 different items and services among 30,000 participants. Registration fee is $15 per year regular, $7.50 per year limited-income membership. Details of terms of trade are left to the barter parties. Lessons range from backgammon to furniture upholstery.

WORK EXCHANGE, INC.
Milwaukee, WI

Organized for and by the senior citizens of the Friedens Church. Director, Marian Wasierski. 300 members. Free. It brings together the elderly and the young.

WEST

AMERICAN BARTER COLLEGE
4365 West Pico Boulevard
Los Angeles, CA
(213) 937-7665

ABC claims 4,000 members in Southern California. Joining fee $150, which is converted to credits in your account. No minimum monthly service charge. 2 to 6 percent fee in cash for each transaction. Membership board to arbitrate complaints. Office in Bangkok for Asian trade.

AMERICAN FRIENDS SERVICE COMMITTEE TRAVELING BUS
2160 Lake Street
San Francisco, CA 94121
(415) 752-7766

"Traveling through small towns, the group provides a mobile and visible meeting place and information–rap center to share energy and bring diverse groups together. It is hoped the new life network can be formed among isolated change groups in northern California, Oregon, Nevada, and Utah."

BLACK BART
234 San José
San Francisco, CA
(415) 647-4593

Sponsors a network coffeehouse on Pine and Bush. Black Bart is interested in work and living alternatives, including bartering.

BRIAR PATCH NETWORK
461 Douglas Street
San Francisco, CA 94114
(415) 647-1120

"We are a network of small businesses that share similar values, one being that we are a business not only for economic return but to learn about ourselves and the world." They send a newsletter to members which contains a skills exchange. Membership fee is $30. Fee is payable by barter.

BUSINESS EXCHANGE
4716 Vineland Avenue
North Hollywood, CA
(213) 877-2161

One of the oldest exchanges in the country. 4,800 members. Service center offices throughout Southern California, eleven states, and Canada, all with reciprocal trading privileges. Fees run $139 the first year, $36 annual dues and 8 percent on all transactions, all payable in cash or chargeable to bank card. Monthly newsletter, hot line, and complete directories several times a year. BX claims over $50 million a year in business for members. Their accounting system uses bank-type checks rather than credit-card systems or triple vouchers. Buyers carry BX checkbooks. Seller mails the BX checks for credit to his or her account. A computerized statement is provided detailing all transactions, including names and amounts at the end of each month. BX has six plans. (1) 100 percent member. Regular retail and service companies. (2) Part-cash member. Regular retail companies that cannot afford to carry the $1,000 BX sales required of the 100 percent BX members. They usually buy and sell using 50 percent cash. (3) Small-unit profit members, such as liquor, groceries, gasoline. They sell for 50 percent cash, buy at 100 percent BX. (4) Large-unit sales, such as general contractors, insurance brokers, automobile dealers. These members negotiate the percentage they accept on each sale. (5) Wholesalers and manufacturers. As the monthly volume of purchases from these members is usually very large, they negotiate the percentage of BX accepted on their sales (usually 20 to 50 percent) and allow them to spend 100 percent BX. (6) Advertising media. Extra commission in BX credit is obtained for sales made. They buy and sell at 100 percent BX.

CALIFORNIA PUBLIC POLICY CENTER
304 South Broadway
Los Angeles, CA 90013
or
1434 Westwood Boulevard
Los Angeles, CA 90024
(213) 628-8888 or (213) 474-4518

Issues a network questionnaire. Its purposes is to provide community groups and issue with listings of individuals who can assist. It is a useful information center for alternative economic policies and research information about the economic development going on in the country today.

COMMON GROUND
461 Douglas Street
San Francisco, CA 94114
(415) 647-1120

"This is a collective effort of growth-oriented groups and individuals advertising what they do. It is free. . . . However different our center and groups may otherwise be, we are all part of an evolving network who share resources by preference as well as by necessity." Advertisers in the directory make available to the public the breakdown of how fees are determined and make available payment options other than C.O.D., including barter.

COMMUNIVERSITY
451 Judah Street
San Francisco, CA 94122
(415) 469-2479

"We sponsor a skilled exchange that lists people's needs, interests, and skills so they can share between them without money. Out of the skills exchange and friends we make, we print a catalogue of group learning situations. We ask for energy and commitment instead of money. People register in person for these courses in different parts of the city."

COMPLIMENTARY TRADE
Los Angeles, CA

Will not give out any information about organization.

CONCINNATION
Los Angeles, CA
(213) 981-3393

Jerry Newmark has organized a sharing community. Through the exchange of feelings, ideas, and mutual aid, he hopes to create an extended family. This family will be the first of many self-created extended families which will then form a community.

EDNOVA INSTITUTE
Berry Creek, CA 95916

A postal school. A full program in alternatives. Time studies, experimental education, creative expression, experimental economics. Each lesson package $2. Will barter.

EXCHANGE ENTERPRISES
159 Haven Avenue
Salt Lake City, UT
(801) 487-1641

A business barter club with franchises around the country.

FAIR TRADERS
North Hollywood, CA

Will not give out any information about organization.

FREE SIG
1623 Grandville Avenue
11-P
Los Angeles, CA 90025
(213) 826-9665

A Mensa society–sponsored labor cooperative. One hundred members, very flexible scheduling and labor hour commitment. A monthly update of new members and their skills and a status report on old members. A $5 registration fee. This is a nonprofit labor coop.

GRAY BEARS
Santa Cruz, CA

A senior citizen activist program that includes a skills exchange.

HILTON EXCHANGE
5032 Lankershim Boulevard
North Hollywood, CA
(213) 877-3681

In business more than twenty-five years. No monthly service directory or statements as cost cutters—just tell them what you need. It's $175 for the first year, $50 annual dues in cash. No minimum service charge but 10 percent in trade for transactions. Mostly 100 percent barter.

INSTITUTE FOR THE STUDY OF ALTERNATIVE LIFE STYLES—
COLLECTIVE RESEARCH COMPANY
P.O. Box 1125
Rohnert Park, CA 94928
(707) 795-1556

"We are an alternative library interested in helping people establish themselves outside the current system."

INTERNATIONAL TRADE EXCHANGE
Los Angeles, CA

Will not give out any information about organization.

LA COALICION SERVICE CENTER
260 Rodriguez
Watsonville, CA

Project Puedo is an organization that uses labor exchange under the auspices of the Service Center.

MUTUAL CREDIT BUYING
6420 Wilshire Boulevard
Los Angeles, CA 90048
(213) 655-1091

One-time initiation fee of $150. MCB "futures" will be debited against applicant's account. A one-time computer account setup fee of $49.50 cash. Charges 8 percent fee on all transactions. Claims 4,500 members in seven states with about 3,000 members in Los Angeles area. Types of members (1) Members who buy and sell 100 percent MCB futures; restricted to members who provide services only. (2) Members who buy and sell at 75 percent MCB futures and 25 percent cash; restricted to members who primarily sell services but also provide some materials. (3) Members who buy and sell at 50 percent futures and 50 percent cash; restricted to those members who sell merchandise and no services. (4) Members who buy and sell at 25 percent futures and 75 percent cash; restricted to those members who sell merchandise on a high-volume, low markup basis. Includes a directory of all members; arbitration committee uses a charge card that works the same way as a credit card.

PEOPLE'S FREEWAY COMMUNITY CENTER
Salt Lake City, UT
(801) 328-4749

A neighborhood council in the inner city that includes among its programs a labor exchange for low-income people.

PORTOLA INSTITUTE

540 Santa Cruz Avenue
Menlo Park, CA 94025

"A nonprofit organization which helps to sponsor networks such as Briar Patch, and which is dedicated to reevaluating economic practices."

SELF DETERMINATION—A PERSONAL/POLITICAL NETWORK

P.O. Box 126
Santa Clara, CA 97052
(408) 984-8134

"We are a network of individuals and groups committed to fostering new forms of community involvement based on our capacity for cooperative self-reliance. Our ultimate purpose is to transform hierarchical and unresponsive institutions into ones whose goal is to enable each person to develop all of his/her potential as a human being." They have developed a resource exchange system to help people all over California share information, experience, and skills. One of their sponsors is John Vasconcellos, chairman of the board, and also a California state assemblyman.

TRADEAMERICARD

777 South Main Street
Orange, CA
(714) 543-8283

More than 650 member merchants. $150 joining fee, no annual dues, 5 percent service fee in cash on transactions. Quarterly newsletter. Dining and entertainment guide. A monthly directory. Four member get-togethers a year. Reciprocal contacts in San Francisco, Hawaii, Florida, and Mexico.

UNITED TRADE CLUB

2156 Alameda
San Jose, CA 95126
(408) 244-2233

United Trade Club has 2,000 members, charges its members $5 a month in cash in addition to its regular service charge, and uses a credit-card system similar to that of BankAmericard.

UNLIMITED BUSINESS EXCHANGE

1246 East Wilmington Avenue
Salt Lake City, UT 84106
(801) 486-9381

A business barter club. Annual dues are $100. Members receive $200 worth of trade credits when they join, which they then work off. No directory is available. Members get monthly list of products and services, but they must call the office to make contact. 500 to 600 members. Referrals earn members $50 in trade credit. Purchases are made with purchase orders, which are then submitted to the exchange within five days of the transaction. 100 percent trade on everything. UBE has nine "licensees." Provides items in trade at UBE store such as clothing, scuba gear, automotive supplies, fertilizer, soil conditioner, wheat.

WILLIAM JAMES WORK COMPANY
904 Center Street
Santa Cruz, CA

An alternative employment agency with a bartering exchange file.

NORTHWEST

CASCADIAN REGIONAL LIBRARY INFORMATION–ACTION
CLEARINGHOUSE
454 Willamette
Box 1492
Eugene, OR 97401
(503) 485-9430

A decentralized group of people affiliated throughout the region, creating an information pool. CAREL has two main objectives: "(1) Publishing a monthly journal which will be sent to organizations and individuals throughout the northwest. The journal will serve as a reliable interchange of communications. (2) To publish an annual northwest network directory to serve as the resource tool for ourselves and others needing information on the cooperative movement in the northwest." CAREL is interested in nonprofit bartering exchanges, exchanging energy and enthusiasm.

COMMUNITY ENERGY BANK
32250 Fox Hollow Road
Eugene, OR 97405
(503) 342-02843

A nonprofit service exchange organized around labor credits and debits. Exchanges occur in several ways. (1) Trading between individuals, one to one, without using the credit hour system—direct trade. (2) Using the credit hours recorded in the CEB system—indirect trade. (3) Combining credit hours and money. (4) Offering an item in trade for other items, credit hours, or money. Members are responsible for signing the liability clause. Membership is $.50 or one-half hour labor per month, both cumulative at six-month intervals.

COMMUNITY ENERGY BANK
Kathy Bing
41 Third Street
Ashland, OR 97520
A nonprofit service exchange.

MUTUAL EXCHANGE
Portland, OR
(503) 292-26624
A businessowners and professional marketing service that uses barter.

NORTHWEST TRADE NETWORK
Halsey Brant
Box 1108
White Fish, MT 59937
A network to link the various collective and labor coops in the northwest area.

PEOPLE'S TRANS SHARE
Portland, OR
Founded by Joe Bentivegna. Nationwide transportation service with 8,200 members. $10 a year for ride referrals. Members must answer a personal questionnaire, be seventeen and up to register. "PTS does not get people rides. We simply provide the information referral service."

SERVICE EXCHANGE
3534 Southeast Main
Portland, OR 97214
(503) 232-0543 or (503) 232-7335
No membership fee. 13,000 members. Contact is made by calling Service Exchange and telling them what you do and what you need done. A nonprofit organization that would like you to contribute 1/10th from each party of the value of the service. Rules: "(1) Don't bite off more than you can chew. (2) Give your phone number to the person you are about to trade with and make sure you have that person's phone number too. (3) If you can't show up for an appointment, call. (4) Most people in our file have been honest and eager. If someone has not done their share after a reasonable amount of time, call us. (6) When you agree to trade with someone, know exactly what each party is going to do before you begin working. If after starting it looks like more work may be necessary, *renegotiate*."

PEOPLE'S YELLOW PAGES

People's Yellow Pages have proliferated across the country. These counterculture and alternative life-style directories are a good source of barter information because very often the listings indicate a receptivity to barter.

ARIZONA

CENTER FOR SOCIAL
 CHANGE
745 East 5th Street
Tucson, AZ 85719
(602) 624-9466
October 1975

PEOPLE'S YELLOW PAGES
9 East 5th Street
Tempe, AZ 85281
(602) 966-0203
March 1975

ARKANSAS

OZARK ACCESS CENTER
Box 506
Eureka Springs, AK 72632
(501) 243-9601
Summer 1976

CALIFORNIA

PEOPLE'S RAINBOW PAGES
Box 363
Venice, CA 90291
(213) 392-3264
July 1975

PEOPLE'S YELLOW PAGES
Box 31292
San Francisco, CA 94131
(415) 282-1913
July 1976

SOMEWHERE ELSE
3144 Lewiston
Berkeley, CA 94705
1975

COLORADO

PEOPLE'S YELLOW PAGES
1460 Pennsylvania Street
Denver CO 90203

CONNECTICUT

SOMETHING NICE
181 Union Street
Bristol, CT 06010
1973

HAWAII

PEOPLE'S YELLOW PAGES
c/o AFSC
2426 Oahu Avenue
Honolulu, HA 96822
(808) 988-6266
September 1975

MASSACHUSETTS

SOUTHERN BERKSHIRE
 COMMUNITY ACTION
Box 582
Great Barrington,
MA 01230
(413) 528-1974
1973

VOCATIONS FOR SOCIAL
 CHANGE
353 Broadway
Cambridge, MA 02139
(617) 661-1570
1976

MICHIGAN

COMMUNITY SWITCHBOARD
621 East William
Ann Arbor, MI 48108
(517) ONE-1111

MISSOURI

KANSAS CITY PEOPLE'S
YELLOW PAGES
Box 10067
Kansas City, MO 64111
(816) 432-0350
1975

LIVINGS 11
6246 Delmar
St. Louis, MO 63130
(314) 725-1607
1975

NEW YORK

BUFFALO PEOPLE'S YELLOW
PAGES
24 South Putnam
Buffalo, NY 14213

ITHACA PEOPLE'S YELLOW
PAGES
Box 385
Ithaca, NY 14850
(605) 272-6820
1976-77

VOCATIONS FOR SOCIAL
CHANGE
713 Monroe Avenue
Rochester, NY 14607
(716) 461-2230
January 1976

OHIO

CINCINNATI PEOPLE'S
YELLOW PAGES
Box 24114
Cincinnati, OH 45224
Winter 1975-76

PENNSYLVANIA

SYNAPSE, INC.
3436 Sansom Street
Philadelphia, PA 19104
(215) BA 4-3359
January 1976

UTAH

PEOPLE'S YELLOW PAGES
OF UTAH
Box 9064
Ogden, UT 84409
Autumn 1975

WASHINGTON

PEOPLE'S YELLOW PAGES
Box 5599
Seattle, WA 98105

VOCATIONS FOR SOCIAL
CHANGE
Fairhaven College
Bellingham, WA 98225
(206) 676-3688

WEST VIRGINIA

ALTERNATIVE VOCATIONS
AND LIFESTYLES CENTER
West Virginia University
Placement Service
Morgantown, WV 26506
(301) 293-2221
1974

Bibliography

Alchian, Armen and William Allen. *Exchange and Production Theory in Use.* Belmont, California: Wadsworth Publishing Co., 1964.

Aristotle. *The Politics.* Middlesex, England: Penguin Books, 1962.

Bateson, Gregory. *Steps to an Ecology of Mind.* New York: Ballantine Books, 1972.

Borsodi, Ralph. *Prosperity and Security: A Study in Realistic Economics.* New York: Harper and Bros., 1938.

Boulding, Kenneth E. *Beyond Economics.* Ann Arbor, Michigan: University of Michigan Press, 1968.

Buber, Martin. *The Writings of Martin Buber.* New York: New American Library, 1956.

Burns, Scott, *Home, Inc.* New York: Doubleday, 1975.

Canadian-American Committee. *Wheat Surpluses and the U.S. Barter Program.* Canada: National Planning Association and Private Planning Association, March 1960.

Caplovitz, David. *Consumers in Trouble: A Study of*

Debtors in Default. New York: Free Press, 1974.

Clavell, James. *King Rat*. New York: Dell, 1962.

Community Market. *Cooperative Catalogue*. New York: Knopf, 1973.

Considine, Bob. *The Remarkable Life of Dr. Armand Hammer*. New York: Harper & Row, 1975.

Cooperative League. *Moving Ahead with Coops*. Chicago: 1967.

Crane, Julia and Michael Angrosino. *Field Projects in Anthropology*. New Jersey: General Learning Press, 1974.

Dalton, George. *Economic Anthropology and Development*. New York: Basic Books, 1971.

Dosher, Anne. "Creating the Network." *The Self-Determination Quarterly Journal*, vol. 1, no. 1, March 1977.

Elgin, Duane and Arnold Mitchell. "Voluntary Simplicity." *The CoEvolution Quarterly*, Summer 1977.

Engels, Frederick. *Socialism: Utopian and Scientific*. New York: International Publishers, 1935.

Evans, Glen. "Bartering—An Idea Whose Time Has Come Back." *Family Circle*, October 18, 1977.

Flanagan, William. "Reintroducing the Barter Economy." *New York*, January 17, 1977.

French, David and Elena French. *Working Communally*. New York: Russell Sage Foundation, 1975.

Friedl, Ernestine. *Women and Men: An Anthropologist's View*. New York: Holt, Rinehart and Winston, 1975.

Goodman, Paul and Percival Goodman. *Communitas*. New York: Vintage, 1947.

Harris, Evelyn. *The Barter Lady: A Woman Farmer Sees It Through*. New York: Doubleday, Doran & Co., 1934.

Heilbroner, Robert L. *The Worldly Philosophers*. New York: Simon and Schuster, 1953.

Heller, Joseph. *Catch-22*. New York: Dell, 1962.

Hess, Karl. *Dear America*. New York: William Morrow, 1975.

————. "Bartering." *The New York Times Magazine*, November 9, 1975.

Herskovits, Melville J. *Economic Anthropology*. New York: Knopf, 1952.

Jacobs, Jane. *The Economy of Cities*. New York: Random House, 1969.

Jencks, Charles. *Modern Movements in Architecture*. New York: Anchor Press/Doubleday, 1973.

Kelley, Edith Summers. *Weeds*. New York: Popular Library, 1972.

Kinkade, Kathleen. *A Walden Two Experiment: The First Five Years of Twin Oaks Community*. New York: William Morrow, 1973.

Klockars, Carl B. *The Professional Fence*. New York: Free Press/Macmillan, 1974.

Kropotkin, Peter. *Memoirs of a Revolutionist*. New York: Grove Press, 1970.

————. *Selected Writings on Anarchism and Revolution*. Cambridge, Massachusetts: M.I.T. Press, 1970.

Lappé, Frances Moore. *Diet for a Small Planet*. New York: Ballantine, 1971.

LeClair, Edward E., Jr. and Harold K. Schneider. *Economic Anthropology*. New York: Holt, Rinehart and Winston, 1968.

"Barter's No Longer Tacky, It's In Now." Part VII. *Los Angeles Times*. May 22, 1977.

Mannheim, Karl. *Ideology and Utopia*. New York: Harcourt, Brace & World, 1964.

Marx, Karl. *Wage-Labour and Capital: Value, Price and Profit*. New York: International Publishers, 1976.

Mauss, Marcel. *The Gift*. New York: W. W. Norton, 1967.

Miller, Henry Western. *The Custom of Barter*. Kansas City, Missouri: Press of Burd and Fletcher, 1900.

Neale, Walter. *Monies in Societies*. California: Chandler & Sharp.

"It's the Newest Trade-off: Bartering Your Services." *The New York Times*, November 18, 1976.

Ott, Gloria Rose. "The Network Exchange System." *The Self-Determination Quarterly Journal,* vol. 1, no. 2, June 1977.

Pirenne, Henri. *Economic and Social History of Medieval Europe.* New York: Harcourt, Brace and World, 1962.

Polanyi, Karl. *The Great Transformation.* Boston: Beacon Press, 1957.

————. *Trade and Market in the Early Empires.* New York: Free Press.

Roszak, Theodore. *The Making of a Counter Culture.* New York: Anchor Books/Doubleday, 1969.

Sari. *How I Turn Junk into Fun and Profit.* California: Wilshire Book Co., 1974.

Schumacher, E. F. *Small Is Beautiful.* New York: Harper & Row, 1973.

Shatz, Marshall S. *The Essential Works of Anarchism.* New York: Bantam, 1971.

Shearer, Derek. *Essays on Economic Democracy.* Los Angeles: California Public Policy Center, 1976.

Sinclair, Upton. *Co-op.* New York: Farrar & Rinehart, 1936.

————. "End Poverty in California." EPIC pamphlet, 1934.

Stinson, Richard J. "The Exeter Affair." *Financial World,* April 17, 1974.

Taxay, Don. *Money of the American Indians and Other Primitive Currencies of the Americas.* New York: Nummus Press, 1970.

Wall Street Journal, January 3, 1977; January 12, 1977; May 18, 1977.

Ward, Colin. *Anarchy in Action.* New York: Harper & Row, 1973.

Woman's Home Companion, August 1923, September 1923, October 1923, March 1925.

Zablocki, Benjamin. *The Joyful Community.* Baltimore, Maryland: Penguin Books, 1971.

Index

147